STORIES OF AN EX-PARTY GIRL

HOW TO FEEL HAPPY AND GOOD ABOUT YOURSELF WITHOUT ALCOHOL AND DRUGS

Danielle "Dani" La Barrie, LCSW, CAP

WP

WALTON
PUBLISHING HOUSE

Walton Publishing House

Copyright © 2020 by Danielle "Dani" La Barrie

Walton Publishing House

Houston, Texas

www.waltonpublishinghouse.com

Printed in the United States of America

Library of Congress Cataloging-in-Publication Data under ISBN: 978-1-7330208-5-5, herein.

DEDICATION:

For my mom, (Muddah Hen) and my dad, (Faddah), and
my closest friends. Thank you for always believing in me
and for supporting me throughout my journey. Words will
never demonstrate the love my heart holds for you.

TABLE OF CONTENTS

CHAPTER 1
I SEE YOU, PRETTY LADY!

Dare to Be Different.

Dare to Stand Alone.

Dare to Have a Purpose True.

Dare to Make It Known.

I remember when life was simple, and my biggest satisfaction was sitting in front of a large plate of homemade baked macaroni and cheese at my grandparents' house. Sundays were always the most entertaining and fun. They were filled with adventurous car rides with my grandfather behind the wheel of his red Toyota car. Hearing my grandmother fussing in her island accent saying, 'Oh gosh, watch it nah!' while my grandfather drove aggressively down the street – was pure enjoyment. I will always remember my childhood innocence. I appreciated everything about my life, my family, and the security of the things I cherished and loved. Those early years were uncomplicated and easy.

Our backyard was filled with my mother's lush green garden and I would ride my bicycle throughout our backyard until I made a little bicycle track/trail. I did what kids loved to do and I loved life without a care in the world. My world, as best as I can remember, was beautiful. It was not a perfect world, and I don't want to paint any false perceptions, but it was perfect for me. My Trinidadian parents, I am sure have a different recollection of that time when there were not many people that looked like us and lived in our small city of Homestead, Florida. I am sure they experienced a different world, with different rules, and different biases, but they protected me as best as they could from the things that could negatively affect my life. My parents offered me a sheltered and quiet life experience until I made my acquaintance with the not so friendly world filled with not so nice kids, and what I perceived as larger than life problems.

Based on my upbringing, I was probably the least likely girl to end up addicted to drugs. I didn't fit the stereotypical "party girl", I wasn't from a broken home or "dysfunctional" childhood, but that still did not keep me from experimenting and messing-up over five years of my life. That picturesque upbringing still did not block me from internalizing the hurts and acting out from the rejection I felt from being an outcast in school and being bullied by mean kids. Despite the love and protection that my home provided, it was school that dealt me an awful blow, and scars that carried throughout my adult years.

I did not know back then there was a better way to deal with my problems. I did not realize the seeds of hurt, anger, and disappointment that would sprout up and grow into rage, bitterness, and addiction. But they did. One by one each pain point showed its ugly face until I was left feeling like I did not have anything to live for. Although I am not proud to admit everything I have done, I am proud that I survived it – because there were many nights that my survival and safety was questionable.

I am not much different than you. When I tell you I get you and I understand you, I really do. I understand hiding the skeletons in the closet. I understand living the double-life. I understand being the party-girl that parties too hard and drinks too much until she passes out. I also understand the woman that wants to do better and be a better person. I understand the woman fighting for her life because she

3

knows that her life purpose has not been fulfilled. I under-stand the woman who wants to be free but at the same time she feels trapped.

The good news is you found me, and I found you through common affinities. As you read this book, I want you to feel safe and comfortable knowing that you have con-nected with someone that fully gets you and can relate to your struggles. We all need each other, and this is one of the things that makes humanity so great. Our ability to connect transcends all our past choices and we can find hope and healing as a sisterhood. I see you, pretty lady, and although you may not feel pretty right now, you will when you finish reading this book.

I want you to do something for me. I want you to take a deep breath, quiet your thoughts, and connect with me. I want you to hug yourself and say, "I'm going to be okay", because you will be. You already are. I want you to write a love letter to yourself and tell yourself how amazing you are. You may not hear it often, and saying it to yourself may seem a bit odd at first but the first person that will love you back to your healthy state is you. I am going to give you the guid-ance you need but you get to take the action steps. Will it be challenging? Of course it will. Nothing worthwhile doesn't come along with challenges. I am not promising you easy. But I am guaranteeing you that when you truly love yourself – unconditionally – you give yourself the permission to break the cycles of destruction that have been holding you back.

As you read through this book you will read many stories about my shadow (or what some people call 'the dark side', ego, inner child; it's the side of me that I consider to get anxious, insecure, jealous, etc.). I am reaching out to you with complete transparency, vulnerability, and honesty as I want you to find the answers you have been seeking. I want you to find your breakthrough. I want you to hang up your wild-out-of-control-party-girl-life and find the true you. I want you to uncover the woman you have buried so deeply inside that you have forgotten who she really is. It is my hope that you renew your soul. I re-introduced myself to myself, (sounds weird, I know) after I became tired of living a double life, smiling during the day while binging and crying through the night. Surprisingly, I wouldn't change anything about my story. I survived reckless drug behavior, alcohol abuse, toxic relationships with men, and an unhealthy love affair with myself. I survived it so that I could live out my life's passion to help women overcome their affinities. I survived it so I could reach back and reach for you.

I have been using this affinity word quite a bit already so let me explain what it is. An affinity is a **very strong** liking for something, and it's not as stigmatized as the word "addiction". I use it to describe addictions to anything such as drugs, alcohol, any abused substance, and sex. These affinities generally overtake our lives when we are suppressed with the business of life, and we do not find a healthy way to deal with the pressures that life brings. When we pretend that we are totally fine and we do not seek out the help we need, we leave an opportunity for those affinities to become our friends. I will explain more about this later.

After battling my own demons, I realized there was not a specific "type" of woman that can become an abuser. Anyone, regardless of their ethnicity – African American, Caucasian, Asian, or their sexual preference – homosexual, heterosexual, or their income bracket – poor, middle-class, or upper class, they can become a victim to negative choices. It is insidious and in general anyone at any stage of their life can have an addiction. "Addiction" sounds so dark though, right? Even when I just wrote it now, it seems so negative; this is why I call it an affinity.

Everyone has an affinity for something, and all affinities are not bad. What I am referring to is doing those things that bring harm to yourself or others. I am referring to those things that you feel you are not in control of, but you feel they have control over you. Let's reflect on that for a moment. Can you think about thing or things you want to stop so badly but you find yourself doing them anyways? Although you promise yourself, "this will be the last time", you find yourself going back for more or picking up the same habits? That is most likely an affinity. Any overindulgence is not healthy for your mind, body, or soul. I hope I am already starting to get you to think. Do not feel overwhelmed trying to process those thoughts right now. As of matter of fact, I want you to place those negative thoughts and emotions to the side as you work on becoming the best you.

As you join me on this journey, I want to set a few ground rules:

Rule # 1: Be Honest. Be really, truly, honest with yourself. Only you know your deepest, darkest secrets. Only you know the skeletons in your closet. There is no need to feel ashamed about ANYTHING. We ALL make mistakes. I am not going to tell you that you need to go tell everyone or anyone anything. Everything here is completely confidential. That is, unless you have thoughts of harming yourself and/or other people. If that is the case, then I would strongly advise you to seek help from the suicide prevention line (1-800-273-8255).

The beauty of you beginning this journey in this way is that *no one* has to know *anything.* Release any tension or anxiety. Which leads me into the next rule …

Rule # 2: Breathe. If any unpleasant emotions surface while reading this book, remember to breathe. Your breath is more powerful than you give it credit for. It is constantly going, keeping you alive, even when you are not thinking about it at all. So, when times get tough (in or out of this book), always remember you can stop whatever you are doing and begin to focus on your breath. In that moment say to yourself, "inhale" as you inhale, and "exhale" as you exhale. Challenge yourself to do this for one minute straight.

Rule # 3: Surrender. You must release and surrender to your process. Be open to receiving whatever life and the universe has to offer. Think about nature – trees grow and flowers blossom…we were meant to thrive. We are complicated plants and hopefully you are drinking enough water every day to keep yourself sustained. We are meant to grow, thrive, and be happy. In order to achieve that state of being, we must practice surrender, letting go, and detachment.

Rule # 4: Forgive. Learn to forgive yourself for the mistakes you have made. From this point forward, if you make a commitment to better yourself and your life, how you are feeling right now or how you have felt in the past, is the worse you will feel. Forgive yourself for the choices that have brought you here to this very point reading this right now. You are enough. You have always been enough. And you will always be enough…I see you. The light you see in me exists in you too. I am just a reflection of you. Those past life experiences you have felt guilty about are over. They happened and none of that is with you right now. It is just you – here in this present moment, right now reading this. You have the ability to reignite your fire. So forgive yourself!

Rule # 5: Be open. Be open to receive and open your internal eyes. Be open to the "coincidences". Be open to the notes from the universe. Be open to kindness. Be open to a warm greeting from someone. Be open to an acknowledgment. Be open to laughter, fun, and dance…without being drunk or high on drugs. Be open to the idea that energy exists, and we are made up of energy. Be open to receive pure joy and love. Be open to receive genuine kindness. Be open to receive authenticity.

These rules are my personal ground rules for my spiritual, mental, and emotional stability, and I want you to apply them to your life as well. You are not alone – we are in this together. Even though our situations may be different, the emotions we have are still the same. We have all felt anger. We have all felt isolated or as if we do not belong. We have all felt unworthy. We have all felt grief or loss. We have all felt abandoned or alone. The more I have delved into my own personal growth, I have learned and realized how much we are all the same.

Allow me to address the white elephant in the room. I know the subject of affinities is not an easy or a pretty subject to discuss. And while we are being totally transparent, I must admit how hard it was for me to write this book. Throughout these pages, I will be sharing some of my darkest moments with you, with the hope that they bring light and love to you. Writing required me to relive through the details of some days and nights I would much rather forget. But I had to do this for me, for you, and those who are stuck in a bad cycle who do not realize they need help yet. I wrote this book with you in mind because before I was where I am today, I did not realize I had a problem. I did not realize how much of what I was doing was affecting me. But I do remember feeling disconnected, empty, unsatisfied, unfulfilled, and unhappy.

You have found a safe place, so let's begin our journey together. Go and hug yourself; you deserve it. The fact that you picked up this book is commendable. It is a sign to the universe, God or whatever you believe in as your divine source, that you're ready for change. Change isn't easy, trust me I totally understand, but change is possible — one baby step at a time.

"The journey of a thousand miles begins with one step."

— Lao Tzu

Chapter Reflections:

- How have you been dealing with challenges?

- What have you noticed is working and not working?

- Of the things not working, what do you have control over that you can shift or change?

- Do you feel like you have been living a double life?

- If so, in what ways do you recognize that you have been doing this?

- What steps are you open and willing to take in moving towards a path of honesty?

- Now that you have an understanding of an 'affinity', do you have any affinities?

- What are the things/habits you overindulge in, in order to cope with the stressors of life?

CHAPTER 2
I LOVE TO SPREAD HAPPINESS

"I've learned that people will forget what you said, people will forget what you did, but people will never forget how you made them feel."

– Maya Angelou

If you ever bump into me you will probably find me smiling and laughing – well honestly, I am mostly laughing at myself and the crazy thoughts that go through my own head. And I'm probably not the only one who does this (yes, I am talking about you). Being a "Happiness Transformation Coach" may seem corny to some but I know the world can use a lot more happiness to drown out the negativity which is so prevalent in our society. I am a licensed psychotherapist with a love for helping others and seeing them overcome the affinities that hinder them from being their best and living their best life...unapologetically. I believe this is the light I bring to the world. It took me some time to form the clarity around how I should show-up in the world every day, but once I discovered it, I made a daily decision to show up big and fully embrace my calling. I did what any genuinely happy person who had been fortunate enough to begin their life again would do, I became a happiness coach. Today I am a professional young woman with a bright career and an amazing happiness coaching platform – and I am unashamed to tell others that I once had a problem with drugs. After I discovered my happiness, I found my strength. I began to love myself. I found my inspiration. Today I have the pleasure of doing what I love – helping people discover the beauty within and giving them the tools to transition through life's adversities with ease.

What is a "Happiness Transformation Coach?" Well, I am glad you asked. But before I explain this let me dispel the myths surrounding this. If you imagine me prancing around sprinkling magic fairy dust like a fairy on people – don't. A happiness coach is someone who helps people discover their light within. I help people understand they are perfect, whole, and complete just as they are. I once had someone tell me that we are all born as diamonds, but when we go through certain life experiences during childhood, the diamond collects scratches and dust. By the time we are adults the diamond is completely covered with soil and dirt. This dirt can come from the irrational or untrue stories we create about ourselves. Having a therapist or coach, going to personal development trainings, reading books, and engaging in similar activities offers us a different perspective about our lives. These activities transform into tools we can use along our journey to seeing the diamond inside. As a happiness coach I am guiding people in getting reconnected. I am helping them 'clean off' and discover their inner diamond. *Shine bright like a diamond.*

Before becoming a happiness coach, I worked primarily in the field of heroin addiction. I remember when I used to hear the word 'addiction', I automatically assumed it referred to a heroin addiction or meth addiction. It was not until I began my journey of getting introspective that I realized how many of my unhealthy patterns were extremely similar to an addiction. These included patterns like jumping from relationship to relationship (impulsivity) and using people or things to fill a void (seeking fulfillment). Addiction is insidious and was one of the biggest reasons I was so unhappy. I asked myself, *what if this is the reason so many other people are unhappy too?* As I began teaching my clients techniques that I began practicing on myself, they would come back and tell me how much it helped them improve the quality of their life. The challenging part of this is there were not too many volunteering and admitting they had an addiction. Not many people wanted to identify with their problems and the other set of people were in denial that they even had a problem. I did not blame them for their decision – the thought of an addiction is scary to face. I knew I wanted to help more people. I wanted to discover a way to bridge the gap and help people find their change. To me it became a simple choice, who doesn't want to be happy, right? Everyone wants happiness and fulfillment, and when I aligned with my purpose, people readily identified me. More and more the title of Happiness Transformation Coach started to resonate, and people started opening up to me. I became a happiness coach because I realized a lot of people do not know the way to reconnect back to their inner light. The light they had when they were a child. Many times I hear "Dani, I don't see how you're so happy all the time" or "you always seem so happy!" I want to teach people they can experience this way of being in their lives as well.

When I was 13 years old, I read about human behavior and psychology, and it really stood out to me. It was then I knew I wanted to help people, but I did not know how. After graduating from college, I went on to work with homeless families, children's hospitals, in-home therapies, and foster care. I have worked in schools with children and with adults, and now I work with drug abuse patients. It was not until recently that I put a fitting title to what I do. I am here to spread happiness – it is what I do and who I am. Happiness is not reserved for some and not for others. It comes down to a commitment of having an awakening or becoming awake. A friend once gave me the analogy of this state as moving from being color blind to seeing color. Happiness comes from a commitment you have to yourself of getting to know who you are as a human being. Through my story, I hope I can be an example for others to not allow media and society to define what happiness is for them. I was once guilty of running around in that hamster wheel, with no idea that happiness could be found in things that are more meaningful. I thought people and things (drugs, shopping, food, etc.) would fill the void. Now I know better…I have discovered my happiness from within.

Proudly today, I spread happiness through my interactions with others. The way I connect to them allows me to see and experience them for who they are. I connect to their inner child, because we all have one inside of us. I look past the facades they put on for others. I see past the "adult" responsibilities. I see through the bad day that they have had, past the judgment, and around the trauma and hurt. How more at peace would you feel if someone saw you this way? This is what I hope to do for you. I connect people to their own happiness. I love giving genuine compliments to others. Almost every time I do, it lifts the mood and lightens the air. I love seeing how people respond. It feels rewarding when they appreciate the compliment because we're all so deep into our phones that we've lost the sense of actually connecting with one another. When I reflect on the idea, I can sum it in these words. **I spread happiness by connecting with the being that is underneath it all.**

The Backstory

I can remember being a woman in hiding and the shame I felt about my life. By the definition of the word success I was successful, in regard to showing up to work every day and being great at what I did. In fact, many of my colleagues and peers knew me as a high achiever. I functioned throughout the day and somehow managed to do my job very well. My outward appearance also sold my perfect life as I was the woman that meticulously dressed herself every morning in high heels, matching necklace, earrings, and bracelet pearls. Accompanied by the cute pencil skirt that stopped at the knees, button down dress shirt, and hair in a neat bun. It was all a lie. The perfect appearance during the day was not the same person that came home at night. I "seemed" so well put together on the outside but inside my mind and my soul, well, that was another story. I was a woman in hiding. I was hurt and broken, and trying to make sense of my life. We do not get to choose our backstory. However, we do get to accept the life, the family, our outward appearance, and make the best of it. I can hear you saying, but Dani, I hate my life, or I wish I had another family. It is okay to feel that way right now. It is okay to feel frustrated with the way things have been. Each of us has our own unique, special light, our inner being – Divine Goddess, that can lead us. Finding your happy place is about getting re-connected to that light and allowing it to guide you to pure joy, peace, and happiness. We will talk more about this throughout the book.

I do not want to give you the impression that connecting to my inner-self and soul was an easy process. It took me years to get to this place. I have made mistakes and messed up along the way. Deep down inside I just knew I couldn't continue teaching my clients about how to get clean and kick their habits when I was doing the very thing I was telling them not to do. I did not want to be a hypocrite any longer. I wanted to be free and liberated. In doing so, I had to ask myself some hard questions. I had to admit that I was not happy with myself. I had to face my truth and ultimately, I discovered my freedom. As you read this book, I invite you to get introspective. Begin asking yourself:

What's my why? What's my purpose? Do I know what that purpose is or what it looks like?

Now it is time to be honest. Are you willing to stay committed to change even when things get really, really, hard? Because life is going to get challenging. You will want to throw your hands up sometimes and just want to retreat to your old ways. "Why am I doing this anyway?" you will ask yourself. For those times, it is going to be important for you to remember your why. The process will seem a little difficult at first – and that is perfectly normal. When you are truly open, God, the Universe, your Higher Power will return it in ways you would have never thought of.

My life transformed when I decided to wake up and start taking accountability. How great would it be to say since that day life has become a bed of roses and I sailed off into the sunset. Well, I cannot say that, because not every day is perfect. Affinities are not easily broken. However, breaking through them is possible for you. If you have ever found yourself in a space of confusion and fear you are not alone. It is not uncommon for professional women to become abusers of drugs and alcohol. It is not uncommon for women to use these vices as an escape from the horrible reality of their lives. I have struggled, and now, at 31 years old, I have learned how critical it is to befriend that shadow rather than suffocate, suppress, or resist it. I have actually named that shadow…her name is Danila. I named her because it helps me to manage her. She will never go away. I learned it is about observing her and recognizing her. It is about me learning how to handle her. If you are unfamiliar with what I'm talking about, keep reading.

Have you ever recognized the side of you that gets jealous, envious, really mean? If so, you have encountered your dark side. It is okay to admit it. Do you know why it is totally okay to admit it? Because we all have that shadow. Every time I have shared this tip it has helped so many women. Recognizing and accepting our shadow is a huge component to our breakthrough. It really makes a world of a difference. I have learned I am most effective when I acknowledge her too. Most of the time Danila just wants to feel heard. So, I acknowledge when she is scared. I acknowledge her when she is really upset, and give her time to cool off and chill. Sometimes, but not nearly as often as she used to, Danila would get the best of me. She would take over with her anxious thoughts and/or insecurities. She would take hold of the driver's seat and begin making decisions, and it wasn't too long before I was in a closet, on the floor crying, as a result of poor/emotional/irrational decisions that I had made. Today, I am so familiar with myself that I can easily and quickly move to what works rather than what does not work. I have learned how to self-soothe and I am so eager to teach you how to do that too.

When I started my "Happiness Program", I implemented my personal experiences to help scope out an authentic curriculum with real solutions to life's everyday problems. I combined "book" with "street" knowledge. I was my own client, for many years. I believe you should know yourself better than anyone else knows you. I also believe that the only person who can shift you is you. I want you to take an analysis of where you are today. Sure, you can continue to read more self-help books making little or no change, or you can decide to finally take action and do something different. I suggest you make a decision to take matters into your own hands, pull yourself up by the bootstraps and change your situation. No one can save you but you. The great news is that things can change, and you are not too late. I was able to break through it and now I want to help you too. In my coaching program, I work with my clients by finding out what their goals are, what they want their life to look like, and we come up with a plan that will work towards getting them to those goals and to that dream. Throughout my program I take my clients through a series of trainings to help them discover the place that feels right for them. I will share some of this with you throughout this book.

It is so rewarding to me when I get to share what I know, and see lives transform. I love it when people sit in one of my workshops, take notes, and then implement. These are the people that are ready to experience a new life. I also realize that everyone will not be a believer in what I do. Maybe while you are reading this book you are a bit skeptical as well. You could be doubting if you can live this "clean" life…and that is okay also. Maybe you have friends and family members who are skeptics that say you will never change. My advice to you is don't buy into what they tell you if their words are negative. Allow them to believe whatever they want, but do not let it affect you. I was watching a documentary recently and they asked the practitioner about skeptics that do not believe in healers and highly sensitive people, or even therapy. The practitioner said he does not focus on the skeptics. He focuses on the person he is working with and helping them feel better. The most rewarding part is, helping people feel better. I totally agree with this.

So, what is your story and can you see yourself in mine? Are you struggling to deal with the urges of your unwanted habits? It is fascinating how when we break through the layers of blockage, we are all so similar to the core. Even though experiences and situations may differ, the emotions are all still connected. Learning how to ride through those wildly unpleasant emotions is probably the hardest part. I always tell my clients, "If you can catch yourself before you get to a five or six on the temperament scale, then you are good…but once you reach seven or eight, it's much harder to bring you back." Side note, that is why it's so important for us to be honest with ourselves and strengthen the side of us that can call us on our shit. However, there is only so much of that we can do. We all have blind spots – hence why having a coach and/or support system is a huge part of success. Anyway, it is important to contain a fire before it spreads. When you are escalating, it's crucial to do things that will calm you back down. I guess you could call it the metaphorical water for the metaphorical fire.

Listen, I know you have been going through a lot, cycling through recurring toxic situations and trying to find yourself. Up until this point, how you have been coping with things has most likely been making you feel worse. I want to help you feel as if life is not happening to you and you are on top of this. I want you to realize that your situation is not controlling you, but you are in control of it. I want to help you get on your feet emotionally and even though the walls may seem as if they are caving in, know that you can breathe and get through this. We can get through this together and I want you to take this journey with me. I would love to help you get there. However, no matter who you decide to let help you, make a promise to invest in a great life coach or therapist or get a mentor involved in your life. You need someone who can be objective and can see your blind spots. Everyone needs a coach. It is very effective, and it gets you to where you desire to go when you have someone that is a support system and guiding you.

I am a firm believer that you know yourself better than anyone else knows you. You know what feels right to you. Follow your heart and intuition to where you should go next.

Although our experiences are quite different, the emotions are the common denominators. I understand the feeling of overwhelm, anxiousness, and stress; it is not a good place. I want you to feel heard and understood. I want to help guide you and help you learn how to follow your inner being and connect with your light. I believe this is what separates me from other therapists and coaches. I combine my educational background and personal experiences to support you in getting you to where you would like to be. I think it is time for you to discover your happy place. Do you?

Chapter Reflections

- Have you created any untrue stories about yourself? Layers of untrue stories that you made up, maybe when you were a child? Stories that you created in childhood and carried into teenage years, then into adult years? Or maybe the stories began in your teenage years and were next carried into adult years?

- Do you recall a time in your life when you "seemed" so well put together on the outside but you knew inside of you was a different story? Has it felt draining? We can feel really drained living a double life.

- Refresher questions:

  What's your why?

  What's your purpose?

  Are you willing to stay committed to change even when things get really, really hard?

- Are you open to naming your shadow? Your "Danila"?

CHAPTER 3
MIRROR, MIRROR

Give yourself to someone worthy, strong, brave, kind, passionate, funny, and sexy.

Give yourself to you!

One day I looked at myself in the mirror and said, "If I keep living like this I am going to die." Admittedly it was one of the lowest moments in my life. I had to be honest with myself. I had to admit that I had a problem and that if I did not find help, nothing would ever change. It is always difficult when we come face to face with the problems we have in our own life. We are generally so good at giving others advice or calling them out on their stuff and would prefer to pretend as if we do not have issues. The reality is, no one is perfect. I, just like you had and still do have issues. I shared with someone about a time in my life when I fell into a deep suicidal depression. They were shocked. 'How could someone like "you" feel depressed? You have a nice car, and you live in a really nice place.' Yes, while this was true, none of those things replaced the day to day issues I faced. It is crazy that we automatically assume that outward things mean that inwardly people are in a good place. I also was guilty about having those beliefs about others, as I watched everyone who seemed to be happy while I secretly compared my life to theirs. I wanted to be like the girl with the perfect guy – *yet I was too co-dependent*. Or the friend with the athletic, toned, built body – *yes, even this was something I thought and sometimes still do, I think there is something wrong with me*. Somehow, I had gotten caught up in thinking everyone else's life was amazing and my life was a total wreck. I had lied to myself repeatedly. The truth is although I was in a dark place – I didn't *really* want to die. I just wanted to stop the pain. I wanted someone to see me for who I really was instead of the person they thought I was.

It was just a matter of time before the negative thoughts of low self-esteem, being different and not being accepted – everything I had struggled with in my childhood would start to play out like a bad song in my life. It took me back to the days when I wore all black and dressed in grunge clothes, sang sad songs, and played the acoustic guitar singing songs with my band called "Trainwreck". Those early years shaped my views about myself. And even more frightening was how I allowed the feelings of a lost little girl to show-up and take control of my adult life.

My Need to Belong

I was the tall, flat chested, skinny girl with no butt in the 7th grade. I had crooked teeth and bottle top glasses – let's just say, I had to grow into my body. While the other girls were fully developed wearing C-cup bras in middle school, I looked like I was wearing training bras. I even stuffed my bra with toilet tissue to create the illusion that I had fuller breasts as I strutted through the hallways wishing the boys would notice me. I desperately wished I could look like the other girls. *Why couldn't my body develop the way theirs did?* I asked myself repeatedly. *Why did I look so different?* I wondered. I hated myself. I hated the way others teased me. My younger years were not too kind to me in the beauty department.

Often, I reflect when the self-hate and low self-esteem started for me. It has been a part of my life for so long that I cannot pinpoint the exact time and date, but I know for sure it started as early as elementary school. Truthfully, it is something I battled with most of my life growing up. When

I looked in the mirror I never liked what I saw. I was picked on repeatedly for being "too" skinny. Culturally being raised by island parents, being "too" skinny was unhealthy. "What's wrong? What's going on with you? You look like you're losing weight! You need to eat," my family would say. Which I unfortunately interpreted as, *What's wrong with me? I look sick, I don't look right.* This may sound strange because many people wish they could be skinny, but people don't realize that skinny people...well, me anyways, I didn't like it. In the same way an overweight person tells themselves they aren't beautiful enough, someone who is really skinny feels this way as well. I looked in the mirror but I never saw a pretty girl, I never saw me.

Honestly, and I have never shared this with anyone before, I secretly admired and wanted to look like Britney Spears and Jessica Simpson. When Jessica Simpson married Nick Lachey, I thought, *how perfect, they're like Barbie and Ken.* My idea of perfect was being "All-American and White" just like the Publix grocery store commercials. I thought to myself, *if I could look like her and have a life like theirs – my life would be amazing.* I wanted to be like Jessica Simpson in the 4th of July Budweiser commercial dressed in a pair of daisy duke shorts, and a red plaid tank-top that tied at the stomach. I was blind to my own beauty because I was so caught up in comparing myself to everyone else. Over time, not only did I tell myself lies, but I believed the lies I internalized – *you're not good enough, you're not pretty enough, you're not smart enough.* No one had any idea of the dark thoughts in my brain, not even my parents.

I was desperately trying to find out who I was. My low self-esteem often landed me in very vulnerable situations with the other kids, especially the mean girls. I wanted to belong. I was an awkward island girl, who was culturally different attended a school full of children who did not look like me and it was hard. I remember asking the girls in elementary school, "Would you be my friend?" in hopes they would accept me. It is a weird and unwanted feeling when you are the last kid to be picked for the team. Couple this obsession with my insane desire to be perfect – it was a recipe for disaster. *Where do I fit in?* I wondered. *Where do I belong?* I asked.

In Maslow's Hierarchy of Needs, it talks about how we need food and shelter; well, a sense of belonging is also a human need. Feeling that you belong is most important in seeing value in life and in coping with intensely painful emotions. We have an inherent desire for a sense of belonging. We thrive on connection; it is what makes us feel happy and secure. Have you ever felt like you did not belong? I am sure I am not alone. According to Maslow's Hierarchy of Basic Needs, Level 3 of the pyramid is love and belonging. "After physiological and safety needs are fulfilled, the third level of human needs are seen to be interpersonal and involves feelings of belongingness. This need is especially strong in childhood and it can override the need for safety as witnessed in children who cling to abusive parents. Deficiencies within this level of Maslow's hierarchy – due to hospitalism, neglect, shunning, ostracism, etc. – can adversely affect the in-

dividual's ability to form and maintain emotionally significant relationships in general."[1] I didn't understand the beliefs I subconsciously created in my head due to this area of
my life where I struggled.

Meet Denise

When I first met Denise in therapy, she shared that when
she was 18 years old, she did some things that she was now
ashamed of. At the time she really did not understand the
gravity of her actions when she became romantically involved with her married supervisor. She was naive and
bought into the lies that he fed her. While they were involved, she thought he was really going to get a divorce from
his wife and marry her. After she had given up everything
for him, she realized he was never going to leave his wife
and he saw her as nothing other than a sex object. She was
so confused and angry, and understandably she wanted to
retaliate against him. As she told me the story she broke
down and cried…a deep, sobbing cry. The kind of cry when
you are so broken and you don't know if you'll ever find
your way. We have all felt that way before…and in that moment I related to her. The guilt and pain of betrayal was
deep, and she felt she was in a dark and lonely place.
Wrapped in my arms was a beautiful woman struggling to
see herself due to the cloudiness of her past. By her outward
appearance she seemed to have it all. Denise was beautiful,
kind, generous, sweet, professional, considerate, and genuine. But she didn't see that in the mirror – the self-judgement
was blocking her from seeing how amazing she was. She saw
herself as a terrible person as she walked in the shame of her

past actions. A past she couldn't change or do over or remove. While working with her, I guided her through practicing how to surrender. Learning to surrender involved learning to let go. Letting go would allow her to finally allow room and energetic space for freedom and for a healthier future. Denise had to have a moment in the mirror.

What she did was so brave! Admitting to the issue and speaking the truth is a major accomplishment and sometimes the hardest thing you will ever do. In that moment of vulnerability, I guided her to gently slow down and breathe her way through it. Not in a forced, "Okay, get over it and stop crying" manner but more like, "That was in the past…it's not here with us or with you right now. He is not here…she is not here…they are not here. It is just you with this breath."

Pause for a moment. It is just you and this breath right now.

I Admitted It

The first time I verbally admitted I had a problem was in a group setting and it was nothing like I had expected. Contrary to the way I had shamed myself in that setting I felt supported. I felt admired. I felt relieved. I felt so free. I felt better. I felt no judgment. I felt embraced. It is my hope to create those feelings I felt that day with everyone I connect with. I would expect that you are reading this book because you are exhausted with the toxic cycles and setbacks. You are over the life you have been living and now you want real change! You have already tried therapists, reading self-help books, practicing yoga, and attending workshops. But even after doing all of that, you have not found the breakthrough you need.

Are you ready to be honest with yourself? Are you ready to look in the mirror? Because honesty is the only way that you are going to make the change. Change will come when there has been an acknowledgement of certain actions and behavior patterns in your life.

Look in the mirror…it is time for you to see yourself. Do not resist what you see. Be at ease and accept it. Embrace it… Everything you see is a part of who you are: Fear, Courage, Sadness, Strength. Now breathe and surrender. We are all encompassing. You are not alone. You are strong. You can get through this. As you pull back the layers you will feel the vulnerability. But rest assured we are a supportive community – we are family.

As a reminder, I stated in chapter 1, this is a non-judgement zone. I firmly believe that having a non-judgement zone is critical for humans to connect and find inner healing. We all have our skeletons, we all have made mistakes, and we all have regrets about some of our choices. Mistakes and life lessons are inevitable, we are human beings. Judgement is interesting, because the very action that someone may be judging you for, may be the very area they may need to work on within themselves, or the area they are lacking.

We all have an affinity for something…what is yours? Are you ready to become honest and look at yourself – even your shadow? Your shadow means acknowledging the actions and characteristics that are not so pleasant to embrace, acknowledge, or own responsibility. I want you to know that it is not always going to be easy, but it is definitely worth it. In order for your life to change, you must be willing to make a complete turnaround. Transformation does not come from doing the same thing over and over again trying to get different results – that's the definition of insanity. Doing the same thinking – using drugs, going from one toxic relationship to another, has put you in the place you are in right now.

Self-reflection is what is going to bring you out. My self-reflection was the key to me deciding that I wanted more. I did not want to be remembered as the woman who had so much potential but could not control her urges, her thoughts, or her vices. I can honestly say there were days that I wanted to end it all. I was tired of drinking and self-medicating. Tired of my superficial friendships. I remember thinking, *I want more…there has to be more than this*, and there was. When I finally made a decision to stop making excuses things changed – it was like my salvation. That day was different.

Chapter Reflections

- How often do you find yourself irrationally comparing yourself to others?

- Do you ever find yourself "just wanting to stop the pain?" What do you do in these times? Are the ways you deal with wanting to stop the pain detrimental to your health?

- What do you do to "fill the voids" of unpleasant emotions? As we talked about in this chapter, some people fill it with alcohol, sex, food, shopping, and unhealthy relationships to name a few examples.

- We all have an affinity for something…what's yours? Are you ready to become honest and take a look at yourself – even your shadow?

CHAPTER 4
THE EMPTY ME

"When our emotional health is in a bad state, so is our level of self-esteem. We have to slow down and deal with what is troubling us, so that we can enjoy the simple joy of being happy and at peace with ourselves."

— Jess C. Scott

Before we proceed further on our journey together, allow me to stop and take a moment to congratulate you on the work you have been doing within yourself over the last few chapters. I am sure it has made you feel a little uncomfortable, and that is nothing to be afraid of. If you are still reading this book and my stories have not dreadfully bored you, or my happiness has not seemed a little too cheesy for you – we're officially a part of time same tribe!

Throughout this book I have shared with you some of the vulnerable times in my life. There is one particular incident that causes me to cringe at the thought of but – I want to share it with you.

Wasted and Lost

It was my birthday and I had plans to celebrate it with my friends at a nightclub in Miami called, Space. I had spent the entire day getting prepared for it, from hair, to make-up, down to the right outfit – I wanted everything to be perfect. I usually did not straighten my hair unless it was for a special occasion because it takes 45 minutes to get it exactly right, but that day I stressed through my beauty process. I also decided to get a facial earlier in the day, which ended up being the worst idea. The facial burned my skin and I had to put on a ton of make-up over burnt skin. By the time my friends arrived I was ready to forget the agonizing preparation and just have a good time.

We planned that I would ride with them going and coming to the party and I would not have to drive. Once we arrived at Space, I was so excited to see everyone. The night-club was full of energy and the music was booming. My friends supported and celebrated with me, arriving and leaving continuously throughout the night. When the group I arrived with were ready to leave, I decided I wanted to stay longer, so they made arrangements for me to ride home with another friend. Somehow, my new ride forgot about me after getting wasted and he ended up leaving me at the club alone. I was too drunk and having too much fun to notice that he had left me behind. Close to the end of the night, one of my guy friends arrived with two of his friends who I had never met before. He realized that most of my friends had already left the club and thought that I probably needed a ride home. He was right! Not realizing the situation I was in until that very moment, I was grateful he pointed it out.

When it was time to leave, I jumped into the car with the three guys and I was so drunk that I could not even remember my address. One of the guys kept asking me what my address was so he could put it into his GPS, but I kept giving him the address to the nightclub. I had memorized it from giving it out to friends earlier in the day. After driving around for quite some time, we miraculously made it to my place. I had forgotten my gate fob, so they dropped me off at the gate entrance and I stumbled my way home. I had put myself in such a stupid and compromising situation. Being in a car with three men, two of which were strangers could have turned out much differently for me. When I came to my senses, I said I would never do that again…but I did.

Emotional Triggers

How many times have you sworn that you're going to stop doing *that thing* (whatever that may be for you) yet you drag yourself, day after day, week after week to the same place you promised yourself you would never visit again? Drugs, alcohol, sex, toxic relationships – the things you know that are pulling you down or holding you back but for some dark reason – you cannot stop. I know the feeling because that used to be my story for over five years. You cry…hoping that you can stop, hoping the pain would go away and somehow those urges would magically disappear. I get it, and I get you. The truth is you are not a bad person and you are not alone. It is time for you to start understanding and exploring your thoughts and triggers, and how they translate into your actions. Living in the moment, and allowing your feelings, emotions, and affinities to lead you will keep you repeating the same cycles.

What would cause me to get so drunk that I would pass out? I often wondered. It wasn't until I began addressing the hurt in my life and talking about the rejection I experienced in my childhood, did I realize there were buried emotional scars and trauma. As far back as my elementary school days, I have experienced rejection. I never felt I was good enough or pretty enough, and I constantly compared by body to the girls that were quickly developing. I remember stuffing bathroom toilet tissue in my bra to appear to have fuller breasts at eight-years-old. This seemed insignificant at the time, but it sowed a negative seed in my subconscious that I was not good enough. It triggered me to want to commit suicide at

13-years-old – and it triggered me to want to end it all on more than one occasion.

We all have emotional triggers. "In short, because we were all children once. When we were growing up, we inevitably experienced pain or suffering that we could not acknowledge and/or deal with sufficiently at the time. So as adults, we typically become triggered by experiences that are reminiscent of these old painful feelings. As a result, we typically turn to a habitual or addictive way of trying to manage the painful feelings." Margaret Hall, PhD[2]

It wasn't until I started addressing the layers of hurt and disappointment of past relationships buried deep within me that I realized I was acting out and making poor and impulsive decisions based on feelings, without being able to control my emotions. My acting out was outward proof that there was an inner problem. Unknowingly, I was seeking validation and approval while bouncing from relationship to relationship, driven by my depression, anxiety, and/or codependency. As I continued on my healing journey, I not only discovered where my emotional pain stemmed from but I was able to recognize the triggers.

This is a good place for me to define triggers. A trigger sets you off in feeling an unpleasant emotion and drives you to do something (act out) to feel better. Triggers set you off to drink…or use drugs…or have sex…or eat…or party. To understand your triggers, you need to be mindful of yourself, which first starts with self-awareness. Self-awareness is the beginning step on the journey to having a deep, connected relationship with ourselves. Self-awareness helps us to understand why we do the things we do and gives us the space to look at what is working, what is not working, and shift ourselves accordingly. In order to understand your triggers, you must pay attention when your mood changes or your energy shifts. Being in-tune with yourself will require you to be present in the moment. When teaching my clients about triggers, I tell them, "as soon as you feel a shift in your energy, pause…back up and think about what made you upset or mad or even happy." Triggers can be activated by anything; people, places, things, or situations. It could be an environment, a picture, or an article of clothing. It could be a color or a smell. The important thing is to be able to identify the shift.

Responding to Triggers

Think about this, when you are hanging out with your friends at a bar, are you more prone to smoke and drink? There is more than a 50% chance that if you are trying to kick a habit and you find yourself in a place where others are participating in that thing, you will find yourself doing it again. Our environment is a trigger, so as you make a decision to become a better you, it will be vital that you separate yourself from the people and activities that are not in alignment of your ultimate goals.

I want to go a little further in how triggers affect our actions. Think about the time someone made you angry and how you responded. You were probably minding your business and they pushed your buttons, right? Now think about the time you received a promotion at work, or you received great news and you decided to celebrate with friends over drinks. That was a positive trigger that prompted a reaction. Notice that triggers can be both positive and negative, but ultimately you get to decide if the way you respond to the trigger is effective or ineffective towards you reaching your goal. I encourage you to take a moment to think about this. Everything in your life has a cause and effect. What are the things that set you off? Is it people? Is it situations?

There are triggers that may have pushed you to the limits and this is why you may find yourself repeating certain behaviors even when you want to stop. Start becoming mindful of when you become upset. If someone cuts you off on the highway and you become enraged – that is a trigger. If you find yourself feeling unfulfilled and you fill those voids with things like alcohol, drugs, food, indiscriminate sex, shopping, or unhealthy relationships – take a moment to analyze what is going on outside and inside of you because these are triggers. Many times if you are not aware of the triggers or the drivers you remain in certain cycles. It is my belief that once you can identify the triggers you can make more self-conscious decisions, in other words, you will not be reactive but proactive. The behaviors you demonstrate are more than likely initiated by a trigger.

Triggers are classified in two different categories: **Internal and External.** I have listed some internal and external triggers below. Although this is not a complete list of every trigger, I am sure you can find at least one you can relate to. Highlight the ones you notice the most in your life.

41

Internal triggers are emotions we feel as a result of an event. They include:

Fear, frustration, guilt, nervousness, happy, inadequate, pressure, depression, insecurity, embarrassment, irritation, sadness, jealousy, boredom, exhaustion, loneliness, anxiousness, resentment, overwhelm, being misunderstood, happiness, excitement, arousal, etc.

External triggers are things that are outside of us that affect how we feel. These are the situations in our environment or surroundings that affect us. They include:

Being home alone or with friends, parties, sporting events, movies, bars and clubs, bachelorette parties, separation, etc.

Let's take a closer look. Have you identified any of your triggers in the list above? Can you identify some of the things that lead you into situations that you later regret?

Take a deeper introspection and journal it below. Make a list of all the issues that make you sad, mad, or anything that leads you back to your unwanted behavior or habit.

Some of my triggers are.........

I notice these triggers when.........

Sometimes there is no way to avoid a trigger. So it's more about learning how to be in it and how to manage it, because sometimes there is no way of fully avoiding it. You can say, "I'm only going to stay at the party until this point," but let's say your ride is now drunk or they leave you behind. How would you handle that? You should prepare yourself ahead of time and know what you are going to do, just in case. Take precautions and have a way to leave or call Uber just in case you are put in a compromising situation. Being better prepared will help you respond better in any situation. Being better informed and strengthening your responses comes from reading books like this one, listening to podcasts, attending workshops, and being actively engaged in your personal growth and development.

Triggers From Social Media

We cannot talk about triggers without speaking on the topic of social media. The pressure to fit in, or be perfect is rising every day, especially with social media being so prevalent in our lives. Because of social media we get a first-hand look at the lives and facades people paint to keep us from knowing what is really occurring behind their closed doors.

They display a perfect life filled with material riches, beautiful bodies, and loving relationships and it causes you to want to have the life they have, while not appreciating your own. Often what you see is not at all what you get. With so many emotionally draining situations in our lives that tug at our affections – family, work, social life, friends – many times it is hard to see through the noise clearly. When I was younger, I can remember my self-image being influenced by the noise with magazines like Teen Vogue and Cosmopolitan. I felt the pressure to look like the models pinned to the pages with their blonde hair, blue eyes, and Abercrombie clothes. Years later, many of those teen stars grew into adults and their stories resurfaced in the latest TMZ gossip with stories about drug addiction, abuse, and violence. The celebrities I idolized were no different than I was, dealing with the same vices and temptations

According to the National Center for Health Research, in 2016, an estimated 44.7 million adults aged 18 or older in the US had a mental illness. Young adults aged 18-25 had the highest prevalence of any mental illness at 22.1% compared to adults aged 26-49 at 21.1% and aged 50 and older at 14.5%.[3] I believe the rise of mental illness is partially attributed to people desiring someone else's life over their own, in turn they struggle with low self-esteem and toxic thoughts. We all have a tendency to compare ourselves to other people…and it's even more blatant on social media platforms. Recently, Facebook depression has surfaced as a description for those children who spend so much time on social media. "A report by the American Academy of Pediatrics defines Facebook depression as "depression that develops when teens and preteens spend time on social media sites and then begin to exhibit classic symptoms of depression due to the intensity of the online world."[4] Whether an adult or a teenager, depression can be triggered when we compare ourselves to what others "portray" to have.

A new study published in the "Journal of Depression and Anxiety" found a link between high usage of social media sites and increased depression. The research, which was funded by the U.S. National Institutes of Health (NIH), involved nearly 1,800 individuals and tracked their usage of nine well-known social media platforms.

"The researchers found that the participants checked into social media an average of 30 times per week for just over an hour per day. Depression testing revealed that approximately one-quarter of the participants were at a high risk of depression. When social media and depression are compared, it was determined that those who used social media the most were about 2.7 times more likely to be depressed than participants who used social media the least."[5]

I have learned over time that comparison is the thief of joy. Danila, my ego, has a tendency to create stories in my mind based off of pictures I see, and I can't tell you how many times I have later found out that the "real story" is actually quite different than what's portrayed on that person's social media. I admit it, I am guilty of it myself. That is why sometimes I will post an unedited, unfiltered picture of myself and a caption letting my heart out, (aka vulnerability post). I do this because people need to be reminded that life is not perfect, and we are all doing our best.

Let's Take Action

Most of us have heard that it takes 90 days before you can make a new habit or break the old. And while this is true, psychologically we tend to feel anything past a few weeks is too long for us to stick to anything. As you begin a new level of self-awareness, I want you to take baby steps and set goals and actions for the next 30 days. If you break this into smaller milestones, it is more likely you will reach your goals. And once you have achieved these, you will have a little bit more momentum to carry yourself for the next two months and even the next year. Taking baby steps, one step at a time, and looking at one area of your life at a time will have a higher success rate. I always suggest to my clients to only take one major life shift at a time. When they get used to one thing and learn how to balance that then moving to another area of life. I have been guilty of overwhelming myself, only to burn myself out and experience resentment. So where are you going to start? Before you think about a new relationship or financial success, let us deal with the most important things like your spiritual wellbeing and your health.

Exercise

Reflect on different areas of your life including: Career, Family, Relationship, Friendships, Financial, Health (exercising, taking care of self), Hobbies/Leisure Activities.

Think about what area of your life you would like to prioritize. Think about the area that you would like to experience the most improvement to and begin with that.

Below are some reflection questions to help you assess where you are and what you need to do to move further. While you take your inner assessment – journal your thoughts.

- What is the area of life you would like to see the most improvement?

- Where are you now in that area of your life?

- Where would you like to be in that area of your life?

- What steps do you need to take to start improving that area of your life?'

- When can you take those steps to start moving in the right direction?

47

Excerpt from Psychology Today, 5 Steps to Managing your Emotional Freedom[6]

Relax – breathe and release the tension in your body.

Detach – clear your mind of all thoughts.

Center – drop your awareness to the center of your body just below your navel.

Focus – choose one keyword that represents how you want to feel in this moment. Breathe in the word and allow yourself to feel the shift.

Stop trying to manage your emotions. Instead, choose to feel something different when an emotion arises. This is how you gain emotional freedom.

Chapter Reflections

- What are some of the things that set you off? Internal? External?

- When you are honest with yourself, do you notice that you tend to put yourself into situations that set you up for failure?

- Jim Rohn says, "We are the average of three to five people we spend our most time with. If the people who you connect with most are not contributing to your soul, is it challenging for you to back away from them and begin connecting with more forward-thinking likeminded individuals?"

CHAPTER 5
I WAS AN ABUSER

"If I make a fool of myself, who cares? I'm not frightened by anyone's perception of me."

— Angelina Jolie

As I got older, I found myself hiding more dark secrets from my family. I worked full-time, attended school full-time, and I had a part-time internship. I had little free time available to hang out but what little time I did have available, I always wanted to be with my friends. This was a huge issue for my parents. My mom would constantly tell me I needed to spend time with the family. I did not want to be around my family anymore. I could not take the rules and restrictions, and I needed to move out...and so I did. Growing up I learned that home problems should stay at home. Well, my home became my mind and the problems stayed in my head. I did not want anyone to know I was addicted to drugs. I was always fearful of people's reactions. I was more concerned at the time of what others would say and not too concerned about my own mental and physical health. I guess you could say I was a people-pleaser, always wanting everyone and everything to be okay. I kept a lot of things in my head and to myself so no one would have to know or bear my burden. My parents were not in agreement with my party lifestyle and I was excited to move out of their house. *Finally, I get to do whatever I want!* I thought.

It was not much longer after the move, I found myself at house parties with people drinking and doing drugs. One of the first house parties I attended, I remember sitting on a couch and I got so drunk and high that the room would not stop spinning, even though I was sitting on the couch. As soon as I stood up, I ran to the bathroom and I vomited all over the floor. It was such a disgusting and humiliating moment. The drugs were provided to me by guys, girls, ex-boy-friends, and they made it convenient enough that I never really needed to find my own drugs, as I was usually with people that already had them or were going to get them. It was interesting how depending on the group of people I was with determined the drugs that were available. Some groups I hung out with wouldn't "do cocaine", so they popped Addys (Adderall). Doing cocaine regularly or even doing it at all is not normal. The drug world was all so fascinating to me. For some groups ecstasy was their drug of choice while others preferred hallucinogens. Some groups were careless about using while others helped prepare you for the come down.

The painful truth was I did not like myself and I lacked confidence, and had low self-esteem and because of this negative mindset, I often doubted myself and constantly sought the approval of people around me. I became addicted to using drugs because it changed my "filter" and gave me what felt like invincible confidence and energy. I would spend hours dancing, taking ecstasy or MDMA (a purer form of ecstasy, also known as "molly") and feeling like I was on top of the world. But as the saying goes, what goes up must come down. Knowing what I know now, I can deeply differentiate that moment was a superficial feeling of confidence; not an authentic one. I was so out of control and partying so hard, I did not even take a moment to eat or drink. Over time I lost weight from not eating and became malnourished. I would completely overexert myself. Doing drugs shuts off your sensory signals so your body has no way of detecting things like body temperature, appetite, etc. On the other hand, it would magnify feelings of joy, confidence, and happiness. Taking the drugs allowed me a temporary escape however, the next morning after the high, I would feel so terrible. The aftereffects of the drugs made me agitated and cranky. I would be in pain and my eyes would hurt; my jaw would hurt and my body would ache from dancing so wild and crazy the night before. It was a roller coaster – the high of spending the night partying and having the time of my life to the low that would be felt the next day when I would wake up incredibly angry, snappy, nasty, mean, argumentative, hating the world, and wanting everyone to just shut up and be quiet. It was so bad. *I am never going to do this again…this is crazy*, I told myself.

Sadly, those crashes did not stop me. I attracted more parties, more drugs, more wild binges, and more blackouts into my life. I started to meet other people that were just like me. They were confused, they felt alone, and they were lost with no idea of who the heck they were. We were kindred spirits. Being in that journey with them was nostalgic. They were not bad people; our connection was genuine. The best way to describe it is, the sort of love that you feel when you were a child and you had that favorite friend of yours and you wanted to spend time hanging out and playing with them. I felt that every day with my group. It was a superficial joy that I could not wait to experience. We would meet up around 7:00 pm and we partied until 6:00 am the next morning. There was no eating…we had no appetite…we just used drugs all night. The time would go by so quickly when we were together. I did not exactly hear these words out loud –

but I am sure my spirit must have been screaming at me. "What the hell are you doing?" I honestly thought when I was using, I was okay. For the first time I was finally connecting with others and the feeling was unexplainable. I enjoyed it – I cannot lie. Using molly was incredible. I would look in the mirror and I looked exactly how I wanted to look – I could not see my acne scars as much, I never experienced my negative self-talk anymore. It made my feelings of self-doubt and low self-worth completely vanish. At the time, I remember thinking I was truly connecting with myself.

We were all seeking answers in our lives, looking to fill the voids and the emptiness. We all just wanted to be free from the voices in our heads, the bad relationships, being misunderstood and rejected. The truth is we were hurting, and we were addicted, and there is no easier way to say it. We created a bond between each other that we believed allowed us to escape. We actually thought we were family, these "friends" and me. It is crazy when you meet other people who want more drugs, it continues to feed your energy in a way that nothing else will. That is what I was looking for when I was taking ecstasy. That is what I was looking for when I was doing cocaine. I did not really like cocaine because it made this drip happen in the back of my throat that felt gross and always made me want to gag. I did it quite a number of times, so I understand the fiending, the jealousy; and I empathize with those emotions. The high was only temporary and once I made it through the ritual, I convinced myself that maybe I felt so horrible because I didn't get enough sleep, not because I had just abused my body close to ten hours. *Next time I will just use another type of drug to feel better. Next time, I'll be more responsible,* I reasoned

Inner-Conflict

I could not hurt my family by admitting I had a problem and needed help, and I could not embarrass my friends by telling the truth. I was stuck in the middle of two worlds. I dealt with the out of control urges and emotional outbursts the best way I knew how – by doing more drugs. I was on a terrible cycle. On the outside I smiled and said the right things to not cause an alarm or magnify I had a problem. I was known as "Ms. Positive" to everyone I knew or interacted with, but inside I cried out for help. Inside I wanted to be free. I was in the middle of it all while simultaneously attending college and learning about methodologies of mental health therapy...how ironic. At one point, I was working as a therapist and partying. I am certainly not here to shame anyone or to make anyone feel bad or guilty about anything they have done in the past. I am here to emphasize I did not fit the stereotype of an abuser. I am not a tattooed person with a ton of piercings – or whatever stereotype they may have for people who have issues with addiction. I mention this not to judge you, but to emphasize the state I was in. I was that very person doing it as well while I was a freaking therapist, with a great childhood, whose parents are amazing and are still married. We all have our things. And it is okay not to be okay.

I am sharing this with you because I believe I finally understand the "secret" to self-fulfillment. The secret to real happiness and pure joy to living a deep, fulfilling, loving, and rewarding life. You know that feeling when you really crave something to eat, and then you get to eat it? It's that feeling – but I feel this way about my life. Most people do not see how we are mindlessly wired to do things to fill that inner hunger or emptiness. Everyone fills it one way or another; either in a healthy way or an unhealthy way. Some people shop and use retail therapy as a way to fill it. Others eat comfort foods – I like to eat a lot of mango or strawberry ice cream, and chocolate chip cookies, as a way to fill it. Some people drink alcohol. Have you ever thought how sad it is that we anxiously wait for Friday, just to get f*cked up and wasted for two days, to come back to Monday miserable and then do the cycle all over again? I know this may seem like a harsh reality but remember this is about looking in the mirror and taking a self-evaluation.

I Am Addicted

As I moved more and more north from my hometown of Homestead, I noticed that things kept getting "closer to home". Some of the drug overdoses that occurred would be friends of mine. It was getting harder for me to cover up my lifestyle. I could not keep hiding and pretending everything was fine with me. I did not know what to do, I was scared and silently falling apart. I could not believe I was hiding in that world – *that dark world*. There were times when I watched former friends of mine totally tweak out on a drug that looked like it could kill you – he literally "got stuck" with his eyes blinking and twitching…and I said nothing. Now I know why many people suffer in silence. They would rather keep the false perception that everything is fine instead of letting anyone know there is a problem.

I was addicted. And the more I coached other professional women I realized that what I was doing was not so rare. One can reach a breaking point in their life where the pressure is so strong that they want to escape. According to data from the latest National Survey on Drug Use and Health (NSDUH), 22.7 million Americans need treatment for a drug or alcohol problem.[7] And although it may sound cliché, addiction truly is a disease that does not discriminate. Benzodiazepines bring on feelings of sedation and are commonly used to treat insomnia, anxiety, and seizure disorders. Due to their euphoric effects, benzodiazepines, like Xanax for example, are frequently abused. We get addicted to being able to escape and that is hard to break. If you are unfamiliar with what benzodiazepines are, they are a kind of depressant or sedative drug. They relax the nervous system. People tend to feel *very* relaxed from them, which is how it can become addicting. This is something that you need a prescription for, however, oftentimes people buy them from other people and abuse them, even though they are not prescribed it.

I had no idea of the rollercoaster that was ahead of me after I moved out on my own. Those nine years were filled with nights of joy, laughter, throwing-up, blackouts, happiness, peace, thoughts of suicide, physical abuse, emotional abuse, and belongingness. As I look back, it baffles me how I was able to hide things from those closest to me. I would have some really crazy days yet my peers would find me "functioning" and going to yoga, grabbing Starbucks, and talking about being happy. I had created an illusion in my mind that there was nothing wrong with what I was doing.

I Had to Quit

I made a healthy decision to find the help I needed and leave that environment of people and things that did not bring me closer to fulfilling my life purpose. When I finally quit, there was a huge void. I had made the long, hard decision of cutting everyone off that I was once doing drugs with and moved to a city where I knew no one. The loneliness that I had spent years running from became overwhelming. I was depressed. There was a period where I didn't have any connections after my decision to stop using drugs. I felt isolated. I felt like I was on an island. I didn't know anyone. No one wanted to know me. My parents lived, what I considered, far away. We did live in the same state but with our schedules it wasn't as convenient anymore for us to spend much time together. And maybe that was just an excuse. I didn't want them to see me like I was. I felt ashamed and broken. I just felt so alone for quite some time. I remember sitting on my couch in my living room in this beautiful city where I didn't know anyone, where I didn't grow up, and all of the nice things I had accumulated didn't matter. I felt so sad. I tried listening to motivational videos. I tried walking my dog, Pooter. I tried meditating. I tried talking to friends. I tried journaling. I tried coloring. I tried taking a bath. I felt like I tried everything. And I still felt so miserable. I was having withdrawals after breaking through the addiction. I forced myself to do something different and somehow dragged myself to events. That was the beginning of my change. I made myself commit to things that I didn't really want to commit to…like exploring things and learning a new environment. I made myself do the things that sounded weird, made myself do the things that sounded strange and felt uncomfortable. But it worked, and I am so proud of myself. Earlier I mentioned self-awareness and the importance of this, as you journey to your freedom. I want you to continue to become mindful of your unwanted behavior resulting in your need for abusive substances.

Reflections: How do you respond and cope with unwanted behavior?

- Do you engage in this behavior particularly when experiencing sadness, anxiety, or other unpleasant feelings?

- Do you think about this activity often?

- Do you find that you can't stop once you have started?

- Do you sometimes lie to loved ones or friends to cover up the behavior?

- Do you make promises to stop but you do not?

- Do you continue to do it in spite of obvious negative consequences?

If you can honestly answer yes to any of these questions, there is a problem and you need to seek help. Depending on how you respond and cope with it in turn determines whether there is an affinity for it. Admitting you have a problem is one of the hardest things you will ever do. As new revelations about yourself start to surface, don't allow the negative and toxic feelings to consume you, allow me to say this to you…

You have it in you. You have the strength mentally, emotionally, and physically to get through this. You are not the only one. You are not alone.

Where you go from this point is entirely up to you. Now that you can look at yourself and admit that you have a problem, which is the first step, you are on the way to the breakthrough you need and deserve. Next, I would strongly suggest you openly admit your affinity to someone you can trust. You will never fight this and win it on your own. Find a counselor or a support group that can help you during this sensitive and vulnerable time. Family is still an option but keep in mind that sometimes family and friends might not be the best fit because they are involved in your life in a significant way. Therefore, it may be difficult for them to give you professional support. There is no easy way to talk to anyone about such a personal problem but trust me you will feel so much better once you admit it. Even if you have previously confessed to having this problem, don't allow the guilt and shame to feed your mind negative words like, "they've heard you say this before so no one is going to believe you." Do it for yourself, and not for anyone else.

There is no pressure for you to be perfect or understand everything that is happening to you in this moment. Breathe and accept where you are right now and together let's look at where you want to be and come up with a plan to get you there. Forgive yourself and free yourself of how you feel others will react towards you when you decide to take charge of your life. More people would find freedom if they would stop living their lives based on what others thought about them. How freeing would it be for you if you expressed yourself through how you dressed, manifested the partner of your desires, traveled when you wanted – without the cares of how others would perceive you? It is true that people expect you to fulfill a certain role, but now you get to do things for yourself…for your well-being.

Chapter Reflections

- Do you feel like you have been hiding what is going on with you from your healthy support system (if you have this) or loved ones because you feel ashamed asking for help?

- Check in with your WHY – remember why you're doing this.

- What are you using as a moral compass? What is your belief system that will support you with your spiritual health? God? Universe? Energy? Mother Earth? Higher Self?

- What are some new things you can do? Networking groups, support groups, or meetups that you can join?

- Have you connected or had the desire to discover what you feel is your passion? Your purpose?

CHAPTER 6
CRY FOR HELP

When you stop chasing the wrong things, you give the right things a
chance to catch you.

— Lolly Daskal

J ennifer reached out to me in the middle of a separation from her husband of eight years. She was 37 years old with two children ages four and eight. She was caught up in a cycle of alcohol and drug abuse and had the tendency to drink wine every night, and sometimes do cocaine with her friends on the weekends. She told me she did it to "have fun and not feel tired." The circle of friends Jennifer hung out with determined the kind of drugs she did. With some friends it was drinking and cocaine, with other friends it was drinking and Adderall. On her weeknights when she was alone, it was drinking and Xanax.

Jennifer's parents had no idea she had a problem with drugs and alcohol, and they were skeptical that "Americans" would say Jennifer had a problem with drinking – her mother being from Puerto Rico and her father being Cuban. There really isn't such a thing as alcoholism in the islands. Her husband knew a different side of her. He had caught her too many times beyond drunk and eventually found out about the cocaine too. Jennifer's parents thought she was getting a divorce because she was being a "bad wife." This was her parents' assumption because they had no idea of the details.

Jennifer admittedly had a problem. Like many women, she was caught in between two worlds; the one she wanted and her reality. Popping pills that she was not prescribed (Xanax or Adderall) was a definite red flag that she had an unhealthy affinity. And just as a side note – some people think that because it is a prescription drug there is no harm in taking it. You can easily become addicted to prescription drugs, and this is especially wrong if it is not your prescription as it was in Jennifer's situation. Once she no longer had access to the prescription drugs she turned to cocaine. It started out casually – only using on someone's birthday. Those one-day birthday celebrations turned into weekend "get-togethers" and that fun habit evolved into full-fledged addictions. Jennifer had gotten herself caught up in the cycle…the crazy cycle that spins your life out of control.

"If you know someone who tries to drown their sorrows, you might tell them that sorrows know how to swim."

— Ann Landers

Addictions can be so insidious. One glass of wine *every* night escalates and becomes one bottle of wine every night. This is not just for anyone addicted to drugs and alcohol. What about food addictions? You say, "I'll just have this one slice of chocolate cake", which then grows into you eating the whole cake and before you know it you're coming down on yourself feeling guilty about overeating. This also applies true to unhealthy relationships. We can easily fall victim to jumping from one toxic relationship to the other or repeating the same cycle of attracting the wrong man in your life. You know he's not good for you, but you would rather settle than to be alone. These decisions in your life start off small and may seem innocent and before you know it, they end up out of control. You cannot fight this monster by feeding it. This is one of the reasons why I emphasize self-awareness. If we are aware of and understand ourselves, we can use caution when we start to veer off path or stop before it is too late. A cry for help generally does not happen until the problem is already very large or almost out of control.

In Jennifer's story, she had a habit of saying she was not going to get involved in an intimate relationship. By this time, she had stopped drinking, and she had stopped using cocaine, Xanax and Adderall. She became actively involved in a recovery program with a sponsor and a home group. Jennifer was doing all of the right things…but she had promised herself that she would only focus on herself until she was emotionally, mentally and spiritually ready to embrace a new relationship. She promised she was going to love herself and spend time getting to know herself again. I was so excited about the love and light she had found within herself. So you can only imagine my surprise when not too long after her epiphany she told me she had met a guy. The distractions began, and Jennifer was back involved with the things she promised herself (and the group) she would stay away from. "Mr. Distraction" shifted her focus and quickly swept her off her feet and back into the chaos. The unhealthy lifestyle began again, and she started back on the path backwards.

Be Honest With Yourself

I encouraged Jennifer not to share things in the group just because it sounded good to her peers, or to me, her therapist and coach. I challenged her to be honest and evaluate every decision by asking herself, "does it lead me closer to or further away from my goals?" This allowed her to really evaluate her decisions rather than labeling them "good" or "bad". We worked on defining and identifying the difference between doing things that supported her in achieving her goals and moving her closer to what she wanted versus doing the things that pulled her further away. She learned to shift the perspective from "good" versus "bad" to "effective" versus "ineffective." Like many women, she had allowed her emotions to lead and persuade her to do things she knew she should stay away from. From there she took the necessary steps to get them under control.

Jennifer is doing well now. I guided her into beginning a journey of getting introspective and connecting with herself through spirituality. We all have the ability to heal ourselves, the guidance and support in learning the tools to do this – that's the key. Today, she has experienced almost a year clean of drinking and using drugs. She is in school studying to become an aesthetician and she is saving money to buy her own home. She even has a better relationship with her parents.

Let's Go Deeper

As we begin our path to self-discovery. I want you to reflect a bit about who you are. What is your story? This is a place most people want to avoid, however, to discover healing and wholeness you must be willing to go to the place you don't want to face. I invite you to shift your perspective about your life. I encourage you to look at your problems as an experience or a lesson. We are all in the classroom of life. Yes, I will admit, some things we would rather have not experienced, but we did, it happened and we cannot change that. From today, I invite you to use your energy to focus on the things that you can change instead of the things you can't. As you think about your story, what does that feel like emotionally? Do you feel angry, depressed, sad? Do you feel lost? Do you feel your heart beating faster when you start to reflect? Take a moment and breathe.

Whether you realize it or not, there are reasons that you do harmful things to yourself and your body. Your emotions are oftentimes associated with the trauma, the hurt, and the disappointment you have experienced in your life. When you do not deal with the root of the issues you can find yourself self-medicating to escape from your reality. Let's be honest – drugs, alcohol, substance abuse – it's just a mental escape. It is a temporary relief from the person you don't want to face in the mirror. We all know too well that if we do not deal with the true underlying person, the little girl inside of us that cries out for help, we will feel even worse about ourselves when the high wears off. I know you can break this pattern if you really want to. I believe in you and expect that if you have been attracted to me, my story, or my energy – it's for a reason. I want to extend my hand to you to offer hope and an assurance that you can break through this thing in your life no matter how hard it may seem. You can finally overcome that vice that has held you hostage and won't allow you to fulfill your destiny and purpose in life. I see you, Pretty Lady. It's time for you to see yourself.

Together let's begin to discuss and understand the why behind what you do. I believe that if you understand the why, then you will easily identify the emotions and behaviors. From there you can find out ways to break through the urges that lead you down the path of self-abuse. I encourage you to keep a positive outlook as you begin to learn more about yourself. It is enlightening to know why we have certain behaviors and to have clarity about what is going on in our head and heart.

Now that you have taken this time for reflection, I invite you to answer the following questions with yes or no.

- ❑ Do you know the signs or patterns where you tend to feel like things are out of control?

- ❑ Do you feel like there is a lot of chaos around you?

- ❑ When you experience that chaos around you, what do you do to cope or handle it?

If you know that you have not been coping in the best way, answer these questions:

- ❑ Are you ready to change?

- ❑ Are you ready for a new life…a better life?

- ❑ Are you ready for a peaceful life?

- ❑ Would you like to have more fulfilling relationships?

- ❑ Is what you're doing effective or ineffective?

- ❑ Does it move you closer to your goals or away from your goals?

Thoughts + Feelings = Action

Through years of studying emotions, Dr. Robert Plutchik, an American psychologist, proposed that there are eight primary emotions that serve as the foundation for all others; joy, sadness, acceptance, disgust, fear, anger, surprise and anticipation (Pollack, 2016). [8]This means that, while it's impossible to fully understand all 34,000 distinguishable emotions, learning how to accurately identify how each of the primary emotions is expressed within you can be empowering. It is especially useful for moments of intense feelings when the mind is unable to remain objective as it operates from its older compartments that deal with the fight or flight response (Watkins, 2014).[9]

Emotion is Energy in Motion

"The Latin derivative for the word emotion, "emotere", literally means energy in motion. It is the feeling sensation and physiological reaction that makes a specific emotion positive or negative" Psychology Today.[10]

Emotions: The feelings that we experience that are fleeting and temporary. Emotions can be pleasant or unpleasant.

Thoughts: Statements that we make in our mind. There is no truth in thought. Everything is perception. We create stories whether they serve us or do not serve us. Thoughts can either be positive and negative.

Negative thought: I am never going to be great at this, or I am not good enough.

Positive thought:I am strong – I can get through this.

Behaviors: These are repetitive actions and patterns. Behaviors are the things we respond to some feeling or thought.

Have your emotions, thoughts, and behaviors been limiting you from moving forward? Is the fear of your past choices clouding your judgment? Refocus your energy from the things that do not serve you to the things that do serve you. Keeping with the reflections above, let's discuss ways we can turn those unpleasant situations into ones those that serve us. Sometimes experiences we think are the most negative, can be utilized as fuel to kickstart the much needed change in our lives. An end to a relationship can lead us to learn to love and build ourselves up. A layoff from work allows us the opportunity to make our dream careers come true by pursuing our own business. I invite you to take some time to reflect on that. Let's shift your perspective. This is also a good place for you to journal some of the thoughts and emotions you are feeling. Go ahead and use this space to release…

After taking a deeper introspection of inventory of myself I feel………

I would like for you to go a bit deeper by utilizing **Plutchik's Wheel of Emotion.**

This wheel will help you pinpoint your exact emotions and give you more of an understanding on where the emotion/feeling comes from. Solving this is a major component to understanding your triggers, and it helps you to gain the clarity needed to help you focus on the solutions, rather than the problems that are causing the dilemma and the intense feelings.

Instructions:

1. Identify a recurring [negative] thought you may have.

2. Look at the inside layer of the wheel and then identify an emotion you experience from that recurring [negative] thought.

3. Next, moving towards the outer layer, further identify how that thought makes you feel. (Do this step again for the last outer layer of the circle.)

Let me explain this more in depth. I had a client named Susan who had the recurring thought, "I'm not smart enough" and "I'm not good enough". I asked Susan what feelings surfaced for her with that thought? She said "sadness." We looked at the pinwheel and started out with "sad" in the middle of the circle and made our way towards the outside of the circle – guilty, ashamed, depressed, lonely, bored, tired; then remorseful, stupid, inferior, isolated, apathetic, sleepy. Looking at the pinwheel together, I asked her do you also feel guilt, shame, depressed, lonely, bored, or tired? Susan would then identify which of those from the pinwheel she experienced and then we would work our way to the outer circle. If she identified her emotions as feeling depressed then more than likely she felt inferior. So now we had the negative *thoughts* and we identified the *feelings*. From there we analyzed which cognitive distortion matched her thoughts of "I'm not smart enough." **Cognitive distortions** are the different ways our brain thinks irrationally.

Once you identify the negative, irrational thoughts and unpleasant emotions you should replace them with corrective thoughts like, "I may not be the best at EVERY single thing, but I'm great at some things that other people may not be good at." With Susan we went into more corrective thoughts and then learned how to apply and practice those corrective thoughts. This process is known as rewiring your brain.

Managing Our Emotions

Emotions are energy in motion. Emotions are temporary and fleeting; they are experiences. I teach my clients how to detach from their emotions. For example, rather than saying "I'm sad", say, "I'm feeling sad", because you are not sadness, you're *feeling* sad. To take this even further, saying, "I'm *experiencing* sadness" is even more empowering than saying "feeling". Now we are acknowledging that it's temporary and it is an experience. This has been effective for many of my clients. Once you practice this distinction then the next step would be to allow yourself time to experience the feeling. We do not want to do this *too* long because then we might sit in it and wallow. After that is complete then you identify what can be done to change your experience? What supports you in feeling better? Experiencing peace, love, happiness, or calm? This is where knowing your tools and coping skills come in.

All or Nothing Thinking: Like "go big or go home". This is irrational because this does not look at the "grey area" or the "in-between".

Magnification: This distortion is making what might be a small situation into a much larger one. For example, "making a mountain out of a molehill".

Catastrophizing: Making a situation seem worse than it really is. This person is best identified as a "drama queen".

Personalization: A person believes that everything others do or say is a direct, personal reaction or attack on them.

Discounting the Positive: A faulty thinking pattern that can contribute to a person's negativity. When a person falls into the cognitive distortion of discounting the positive, they overlook their personal achievements and disregard their positive attributes.

Emotional reasoning: Making decisions solely on emotions, without any logical thinking.

Another example: If you have a thought like, "I'm not smart enough", the feelings that usually come with this are sad, ashamed, feeling inferior, or angry. This cognitive distortion would be considered discounting the positive. I am sure there have been times when you have known things that other people did not know. This would prove that feeling to be false. This logic is also based on emotional reasoning – reasoning based on emotions. In order to correct this thought, you would change "I'm not smart enough" to "I may not be the best at everything but I am extremely good at some things."

Negative thought:	Feeling:	Cognitive Distortion:	Corresponding Thought:
"I'm not smart enough"	Sad, ashamed, inferior, mad	"Discounting the positive, emotional reasoning"	"I may not be the best at **every**thing, but I am extremely good at some things."

Pause and Reflect.

After going through the wheel are you better able to see just how much your thoughts affect your feelings? And then based on your thoughts and feelings, can you see how your actions tend to be based on those thoughts and feelings? It is important to see this, because if you learn how to shift those thoughts and the negative things you say to yourself, you will be better able to take action in a way that will create a happier, fulfilling lifestyle, because now your actions and behavior is based on rational, positive thinking rather than negative irrational thinking.

Hey Pretty Lady, I want to check in with you. I know things may seem like a lot right now. Changing your habits, thoughts, friends…it can feel like a mental overload. Take it one step and one thing at a time. Always remember WHY you are doing this. If this were easy, everyone would be doing it. Imagine the life you can have and the *possibilities.* Imagine the liberation, harmony, freedom, and peace. Embody the feelings of peace and love. Embody the feelings that you are longing to experience. This will help remind you why you are doing this. Remember to breathe. As long as you keep moving forward, no matter the pace, you're still moving. Keep going, you will reach your desired destination.

Chapter Reflections:

- Do you recognize a shift that occurred in your commitment to getting every day responsibilities done? Do you find that your affinity started as just a "once in a while thing" and then turned into a regular habit?

- Have you recently experienced something that seems overwhelmingly "negative"? Almost as though you're not sure how you're going to get yourself out of it? In what ways can you attempt to shift your perspective. Rewrite the narrative in your head. How can you get present to what is in front of you without getting lost in your thoughts?

- Practice noticing your thoughts as well as noticing if they are based on facts or feelings. If they are based on feelings, then very likely your thoughts may be irrational. Take a moment to skim over the cognitive distortions during times when you are feeling extremely sad, anxious, doubtful, scared, insecure, ashamed, or any other "negative" (low frequency) feelings.

- Check in with your WHY – remember why you are doing this. Acknowledge yourself for the awareness you have gained thus far.

STORIES OF AN EX PARTY GIRL

CHAPTER 7
HOW DO I GET OUT
OF THIS ANYWAY?

*"Your net worth to the world is usually determined by what remains
after your bad habits are subtracted from your good ones."*

— Benjamin Franklin

As you have been reading this book you have probably thought to yourself – "this all sounds great, Dani, I want to change, but how do I get out of this anyways? If I leave this life, these friends, and everything that is familiar… What will I do? Where will I go? Will I have to start over?" Here is a perfect time to breathe. I do not want you to become overwhelmed with everything. Remember to keep telling yourself you do not have to figure every single detail out. You do not need all the answers. The universe will release to you the things necessary to complete your journey. You simply must trust the process and know that everything will work out. And although those are all great and valid questions you may have, there is no specific or right answer that fits everyone. You will find something that works best for you to help you achieve your goals. Remember each person's process is different. To help you get started let me provide you with some direction and tools to start you on your journey by including some things that have personally worked for me and the clients that I coach.

Do not pressure yourself and try to fix your entire life in the next 30 days. That is not realistic and if you shock your brain into thinking everything is changing and your whole world is falling apart, you will end up in remission. It is best that you make baby steps. Allow yourself the freedom to change and adjust. We often get stuck in the routines and we feel like this is just who we are, but that's not true. You can improve your life at any time. The unfulfillment you feel is your sign from the universe that there is more to life than what you are living. Sometimes we do not realize how far off

STORIES OF AN EX-PARTY GIRL

the path we are because we have been off so long that it becomes a new normal. You know that you feel unfulfilled, but you don't know how to fill the void. This is your sign to keep seeking, keep moving, and keep believing things will work out for you.

"It's never too late to become who you want to be. I hope you live a life that you're proud of, and if you find that you're not, I hope you have the strength to start over."

— F. Scott Fitzgerald

Mindset

Your mindset will determine how successful and effective you are in making the necessary changes. Your mind will also determine how quickly or how slowly you will implement the required steps. If you cannot first see the change in your mind, you will never see the change take place in your life. According to work by pioneering Stanford psychologist, Carol Dweck and others, the best predictor of success in life is none of these usual suspects – it's your mindset.[11] Those who achieve great things generally believe they can improve, learn to grow, and elevate their mind. From today, I want you to start refocusing your mind to see yourself getting free from the affinities. See yourself living a life of freedom and peace. What I mean by that is you can close your eyes for a moment and mentally take yourself to a happy place. Go ahead and take a moment to do that right now. As you see that place in your mind, begin to breathe slowly, and relax. Stay in that moment. What does that happy place look like for you? What does it feel like? What does it smell like? Can you see yourself living in that place – the place of freedom, fulfillment, and happiness daily? If you can see it first in your mind, you can follow the actions necessary to get you there. I spend a lot of time in meditation – stilling my mind and calming my spirit so that I can constantly be in-tune with that place. As you continue to meditate you will manifest the life that you want.

Fear of New Beginnings

I used to be afraid of new beginnings – well, any sane person will most likely feel this way. A new beginning is best compared to the monster in the closet that we fear as kids – although we have never actually seen this so-called monster, we just know he is in there. *Or is he?* When I was younger, I was in the gifted program, so often it required that I change schools, which meant I had to meet a new set of friends in a new environment. I was always anxious about meeting new people, not because I did not enjoy meeting them, I was always a warm and welcoming person. One thing I have always thrived on is human connection. I developed that habit in middle school of always wanting to hug people as my way of saying "hello" and it sort of became an expected thing of me. If you saw me coming, I was giving you a hello hug. Anyone in my path was a candidate for the hug. Well, I will never forget the day a girl told me, "I was the most fake person and who gives *everyone* a hug hello?" she mocked. I was shattered. It was the first time that I can remember I had finally built up enough courage to be loving to others externally, and someone intentionally hurt me for it. I was shamed for being "too friendly", which was interpreted as me being fake. I felt embarrassed by the way others responded to me and my pure intentions were laughed at.

Many of us have that little girl inside of us and are afraid of how we will be perceived and judged. It would be crazy for me to say from here on, every new environment will be warm and inviting for you. We both know that is not realistic. However, I will say that once you find your community of people that understand you and that you can relate to, I believe that your life will drastically improve for the better. Most of us are creatures of habit and anything that takes us out of that zone causes fear and anxiety. I felt that way for a long time when I wanted to quit using. I knew there was more to life than drinking and drugs, but I did not know if I was strong enough to take the journey alone. I felt that loneliness and rejection quite often at a young age and I surely did not want to revisit that dark and lonely place again. Sometimes when you think about starting over you feel like you are looking down a black hole. Fear is one of those things you must face. We have all been there. The only way to defeat it is to take a step forward. The shift is going to be scary and you will feel disconnected, because you are switching to something that you are not used to doing but it can be fun – it's all based on your perspective. In all transparency it is going to be difficult to make the adjustment but remember your why.

Environment Change

This is probably one of the areas where I receive the most push back with the women I coach. Let me go ahead and address the white elephant in the room. Yes, change is a requirement to break any affinity. Yes, change in your environment means that you get to change who you spend the most time with. There may be some friends that you continue to spend time with but not all of them, and definitely not the ones who influence you to exhibit the behavior you are trying to change. You may need to switch the places you go. You will need to be careful of who and what you are around, to avoid the triggers that we talked about in previous chapters. But please do not freak out on me. You can do this...you've got this. Go ahead, take a deep breath, let it out with a sigh, and say, **I can handle it.** If you do not change your environment, you will remain in the cycle that you're in right now. Go ahead and reinvent yourself.

"Our environment dictates what we choose to do, as opposed to what we want to do. If you have choices around you that are distracting or leading you to undesirable outcomes, then it becomes hard to make the right choices. On the flip side, having an environment that only has desirable choices constricts you to do what's important for yourself." *Why Your Environment is the Biggest Factor in Changing Your Life by Melissa Chu.*[12]

My Process

My new awareness came after one of those in-my-own-head conversations; an epic moment when I said to myself...*Hmmm...this meditation seems to be working for my clients, maybe I should try it too.* I started by personally implementing the techniques I taught my clients, and the meditation methods worked for me too. There was a noticeable change in my behavior, my mood, and my mindset. I experienced more balance – emotionally, mentally and spiritually. I thought it would be good if I could start meeting people that incorporated these techniques in their daily routines as well. I started going to yoga classes and festivals, and participated in activities that not only replaced the ineffective habits, it allowed me an opportunity to meet new people and make new friends.

Steps to Overcome the Affinity:

Step # 1: Identify Your Why

Why do you want to break the habit? Is it limiting you from living a fulfilling life? Knowing your "why" is critical. Being fully aware and connected to your why will help you when staying focused gets hard. You will need to clearly define what this means to you, as everyone's why is different.

Step # 2: Set Your Boundaries and Moral Values

What is your moral compass? How do you decide what is the right or the wrong thing to do? Does your moral compass lead or guide your decision-making? Whether we realize it or not we all have a moral compass. These are your set of values that were most likely defined for you as a child by your family – they are your foundation. Use these to set the boundaries of what you will or will not do, and what you will or will not allow in your environment.

Step # 3: Explore New Things

Discover things to experience and do what makes you feel genuinely happy. Joining networking groups, support groups, or meetups that are of interest to you is critical. Replace the unpleasant things or ineffective habits with pleasant ones. It is a great and fun way to meet new, like-minded people but it's also the best way to stay accountable on your journey.

Step # 4: Reconnect to your purpose

You were created for a reason. It doesn't matter how you started, it matters how you finish. If you would be honest with yourself, you will probably admit there is still something inside of you desire to do. There is something that still makes you light up on the inside – this is the thing I want you to reconnect to again. This does not have anything to do with anyone else. What do you want to do with your life? We all have a purpose in life and it is our purpose that drives us to desire more and to be more. It is not too late for you to discover and uncover what this is for you. Make it a daily routine to envision the life that you desire. See yourself being a blessing to other people and your life having so much meaning. See it first and then start to live it.

Step # 5: Fight for it!

Fight for the life you want. Fight for the life you deserve. When I say, "fight" I do not mean with others, this is a battle within yourself. Fight for the dreams that have not yet come true and for your legacy. You have been in your own way all this time. This fight is worth it. This journey won't be easy and there are times you'll want to throw your hands in the air, cry, and/or give up. Fight for yourself. No one else can fight for you.

I want to take a moment and acknowledge you for coming this far. Up until this point we have identified mental and emotional health, triggers – internal and external. We've also looked at stepping back and taking a look at how we perceive things, and now we have faced the addiction head on. From this day forward you get to choose to change. I say "get to" rather than "have to" because technically you don't *have to* do anything. You're always at your own will here. There will be days where you will feel like you're starting all over again. But if you've come this far, you've built a firm foundation and you're only building on top of that. *I see you **Pretty Lady**.*

Social Connections

"Connection is the energy that exists between people when they feel seen, heard and valued, when they can give and receive without judgement, and when they derive sustenance and strength from the relationship." — Brené Brown

One of the reasons I used drugs was because of the social connection. I deeply missed that when I became sober. When I expanded my horizon to meet new friends, I was able to make new connections with people who have life goals and similar interests that I do. Those like-minded people have turned into great friends and support that I have made since overcoming and breaking through the addiction. I honestly do not miss my old life. Sure, I love all of my old friends, but I wasn't happy with that Dani. I replaced binging on weekends to brunching with people that understand me and where I'm headed. I have brunch with one of my friends every Sunday, who was once in a similar situation, where everybody around her was using as well. She and I understand each other, and we keep each other accountable. We get along so well because we have those things in common. We share our morning routines, our funny stories, and the latest podcasts. I continue to want to do better because of these positive people in my life. Our relationship has evolved from both of us wanting more for ourselves and not wanting to be around the people that were using. I am convinced the universe brought her into my life because I made a decision that I wanted to live a purposeful and fulfilling life.

Continue to take inventory on yourself. Find out who you are and what you enjoy doing; what makes you happy will be pivotal for you. I want to assure you there are alternatives to doing things that have brought harm to you in the past. If you would be willing to embrace them you will find yourself enjoying life. There are some things I invite you to think about as you make this transition.

Get in Touch With Your Higher Power: Having a spiritual connection with God, the Spirit, or your Divine Power is the foundation you need. This connection will not only guide you, but you can also connect to this source when you need strength to keep going. We all need this help. Make it a daily practice to be calm, be still, and listen as your Divine Power guides you.

Get Connected to Your Core Value System: Above everything else, you must know yourself and be true to who you genuinely are. Until you know this, you will not be able to experience your breakthrough. Think about the thing that makes you happy…do you still do it? If not, why not? When did you disconnect from that place? Sometimes it is good to go back to the place that you felt your best. If you cannot physically travel back there, take a mental trip there. Connect with the true essence of you.

As you continue your journey remember that what you surround yourself with will either help and encourage you or limit you from reaching your goals. As humans we are subject to take on the attributes of the people, things, and situations that we spend most of our time with. When I tell my clients to leave their environment, it's because I know whatever they see, touch, and smell, they will replicate. This may seem hard for you at first. I know that feeling your way out in the darkness of life may make you feel alone. This is where having a support system comes in. There are better choices available for you and I think that sometimes we are afraid that other choices may not feel as good as the affinity we have. When you start to do new things, and embrace the new you, you will discover there may be a better choice, and you are guaranteed to feel better about yourself when you do it.

The Alternatives

Health and Exercise: Having a healthy body will help you have a healthy mindset and will help you make better decisions. Keep in mind if you stay with a community of people, online or offline, who are supporting and on the journey with you, you will have a higher percentage of sticking to it.

Self-Care: Self-care is a physical and spiritual act. When you take care of yourself, you send a message to the universe that you value who you are. When you take the time to put the necessary time and attention to rejuvenate your mind, body, and spirit, you send a message that you are worth it. When you start believing this, the energy will send this message to others around you.

Hobbies: Challenge yourself to do something new. It can be as vigorous as learning Tai-Chi or something as calm as knitting. Do some sort of activity that takes your mind off the day to day stresses of life. Taking time to relax and engage in an enjoyable activity can help benefit your mental health. Hobbies help improve a person's sense of identity, usefulness, and wellbeing, and eliminate feelings of worthlessness and self-doubt.

Explore the World and Travel: You will be amazed at how standing on the beach will rejuvenate you or how standing on the peak of a mountaintop will excite your senses and give you a rush of adrenaline. Make yourself a bucket list, watch the travel channel, and start planning out your next adventure. There are many groups for travel that you can join and meet new people. Try your local meet-up to start. From there, challenge yourself to go global.

Join a Community: Having some sort of support system in place is vital. Growth happens on the other side of our comfort zone. If we can relate to others on the same path, we are more than likely to stick to it. Being a part of a community increases our chances of success. Our community will hold us accountable. The stronger the support system, the more we can move through those challenges with ease and grace.

Chapter Recap

- What do you see as your purpose? What challenges have you gone through and overcame in your life? How can you use your knowledge and experience of this to help other people?

- Higher Power does not necessarily have to be a specific religion. A Higher Power can be nature, energy, the Universe…a Higher Power can be whatever that looks like or feels like to you.

- Define your core value system? What do you value most in your life? What sorts of experiences would you like to manifest or attract if you could?

- Have you considered joining a community (or communities) that are in alignment with what you desire for your life? Surrounding yourself with like-minded people will help keep you on track to creating a life of inner peace and joy, especially when times get challenging.

CHAPTER 8
FREEDOM

To know yourself as the being underneath the thinker, the stillness underneath the mental noise, the love and joy underneath the pain, is freedom, salvation, enlightenment.

— Eckhart Tolle

It is my desire that you will unveil your true freedom as well. It is my desire that you discover your wings and soar high above where you are today to the place that you are going. This is true freedom. This is what you should be striving for. I have unlocked the keys to my freedom and happiness, and I never want to go back to the woman that was so depressed that she cried for days straight. The memory of the dark place drives me to continue becoming a better version of me. I can't say that everyone will experience true freedom but it is my hope that you will. It is the most liberating experience. I am free from the limitations others may try to place on me. I am free to make decisions that serve my purpose on Earth. I am free to choose what I intake in my body. Each day I wake up, I feel refreshed, and renewed to live my life. I move uninhibited by anything that will try and tell me anything that goes against the positive things that I speak to myself. I refuse to listen to anyone who will tell me that I am not deserving of living the life I dream about.

The dictionary defines freedom as, "the right to act, speak, or think as one wants without hindrance or restraint." [13] My definition of freedom is feeling liberated in all areas of your life, having balance, and not feeling trapped. Freedom is something we should all strive to attain. When we think about the struggle different cultures have endured fighting for their freedom, it tells us how important freedom is. The only person who can stop your freedom is you. When you are under the control of an addiction you are not free. If you cannot control yourself or tell yourself "no", that is proof that you don't have freedom. Your decisions are driven by how free you really are.

Forgive and Grow

Freedom and forgiveness – two powerful words that are critical to living our most positive lives possible. Allow yourself the freedom to forgive and grow. You can never truly experience freedom until you learn to forgive and take ownership. Before we go any further, I invite you to think about who you need to forgive as you start to walk into your transformed life. Aside from forgiving others, we also need to forgive ourselves. We have all been guilty of blaming ourselves for the actions we took. There is a difference between taking ownership for your actions and feeling guilty and hard on yourself that you never fully heal and recover. I encourage you to take some time to really sit and think about who you need to forgive. It is time for you to make some changes for the better and you do not need to carry any unnecessary baggage with you. Once you forgive, move on and grow! Take a deep breath – and speak this out loud.

I forgive _____ (add your list here).

Living a Limitless Life

Freedom means living a life of no limits, no walls, and nothing holding you back. It is being in control of your life rather than your life controlling you – you are on top of it instead of the other way around. Freedom feels like you can come and go as you please. You have the confidence and you can stay grounded no matter where you go because you are not chained by anything or anyone. To me freedom is not just a physical state, but it is a spiritual and emotional state as well. It is total liberation. Being connected so deeply to yourself and to a higher power is powerful. It is being able to rely on that relationship. It makes you feel strong because you know no matter what, the Universe has your back. Freedom transcends spiritually and emotionally as well.

How do you define freedom? What does it look like? What does it feel like? What are some of the things that come to your mind when you think of freedom? **Go ahead and journal that here.**

Now read aloud what you wrote above. Are you living that life right now? If you answered yes – congratulations. If no, what do you need to change today to start moving forward in that direction?

I can guarantee once you clearly define what freedom means to you, no one or nothing will be able to keep you from experiencing it. Think about the animals in the wild. Once they are set free they are wise enough to never be captured or held hostage again. See yourself being this free.

Gratitude

Being appreciative of where you are right now and what you have, will open the laws of abundance in your life. Freedom is also gratitude. Gratitude is having an appreciation for whatever the Universe, God, or your Higher Power has granted you or has allowed you to experience. It is truly recognizing and connecting with the feeling of being grateful. So many people take life for granted. But what would you do if you really did not have certain things anymore? Like your legs? Or eyesight? Or even a roof over your head? What if tomorrow you lost something or someone you valued and loved?

When I was 16, I was in a terrible car accident and my outlook on the appreciation of life was tested. Earlier that evening, I was at a girlfriend's house listening to music while she finished getting ready with plans to attend a dance at her school. Once she was done getting ready, we got in my car and drove to her friend's house to also pick him up and carpool together. After we picked him up, we discovered he had forgotten the tickets for the dance. When we realized this, we hurried back to pick the tickets up and as I made the U-turn to head back, a truck completely T-boned the side of my car and pinned me to the car. It was such a terrible scene; I do not know how they managed to cut me out of the car. I remember crying and saying, "I don't have the money for this," to the paramedics as they were cutting my car apart to get me out of it. I do not really remember too much of the ambulance ride but I do remember at some point, opening my eyes and looking up, and the hospital lights being bright. The hospital visit was a blur, I am sure they had me heavily medicated to help ease the pain. When I finally left the hospital, I did not leave walking or being able to stand up, I was in a wheelchair. I also remember chipping off a piece of my car paint (it was a dark red Mitsubishi Mirage) and holding on to it. I think it was my way to hold on to the memory of my very first car. When I returned to school, I told my high school friends about my car accident and showed them a picture of the totaled car along with the paint chip I had. Thankfully, I was able to recover without any physical scarring. I know that there are others who did not walk away from their tragic accidents. Since that day I have had an immense appreciation for life. It was like I had escaped death.

Imagine if things changed completely for you and everything familiar to you was destroyed or taken away. Sadly, this is an everyday reality for some people. I have sat in therapists' groups in the past where they instruct the clients to create a gratitude list and in less than five minutes the attendees are finished...some even quicker. They list I am thankful for my health, my parents, my dog, my partner, a family member or a best friend; they just run off the list without much thought. I can tell they do not really stop and put their mind, their body, or their energy into what it would be like if things in their life were to really change for them suddenly. When someone really *embodies* those emotions, that to me is gratitude.

At this point in my career I have interacted with thousands of people and I have heard some tragic stories. People have endured some extremely unimaginable, painful, and emotional experiences, my heart breaks for them. Their experiences remind me that I have so much to be grateful for. Working in addiction treatment centers, I am constantly exposed to death. I can meet with someone on a Friday and leave for the weekend, come back by Tuesday, not only has the person left against therapeutic and medical advice but they overdosed and passed away. This would happen so often. I must admit that even today it is hard for me. It has gotten a little easier, in the sense that I am becoming a little bit desensitized. But it is still that shock, there's always that initial shock.

Life is precious, we should all be learning to be thankful for everything – big and small. We have the freedom that many people would want. Be grateful for the things you may take for granted. Be grateful that we can breathe. Be grateful for eyesight. Be grateful to be able to taste things, to talk to people, to communicate with them. Be grateful for having a roof over your head. Be grateful for having food in your stomach and if you are hungry, I am sure you have access to getting food. Be grateful for where you are today. Be grateful for how far you have come. Be grateful for all the experiences you have been through and all of the lessons that you have learned in your life thus far.

Gratitude Journal

If you haven't started a gratitude journal, I encourage you to start keeping one. I like to write in mine daily, but if you cannot commit to daily at least try to write in it a few times a week. Keeping this journal will help you stay focused on the important things in life and it will keep you grounded. You will notice that keeping a journal will also help you to become more positive. People underestimate the power of writing. Sometimes clients of mine shy away from it because they do not think it will do much…but it does. If you do not already journal or have a journal, I encourage you to get one that you really like, whether that's logistically or aesthetically. Having a journal you're excited about will support you in writing in it, rather than buying any kind of notebook. Having a gratitude journal is great for me. It really improves my mood. I use it to sit, think, and reflect. The calmness it creates for me keeps me centered. I love it. I noticed a real improvement in my overall wellbeing ever since I started writing in it. When I write, I sit and I reflect.

Reminders and Routines

This is my modern-day tip. Ten years ago, this would not have been necessary but with the busyness of our lives today we need reminders. One tool I suggest is setting an alarm; that seems to be the most effective for a lot of people. Using your phone, set an alarm on your phone named 'Gratitude' and set multiple alarms throughout the day as reminders. Every time your alarm goes off, think about the things you are grateful for in that moment. Setting an alarm and/or reminding yourself of the things you already have in your life on a regular basis has been shown to improve mood and depression. This is just one suggestion. You can use any type of alarm and it doesn't necessarily have to be a phone alarm. If you hear a bird outside or plane go by or a child crying or laughing, that can be a reminder to be grateful. Some people wear something on them as a reminder to be in a state of gratitude or to stay grounded like meditation beads or bracelets. Do whatever resonates with you.

Morning and evening routines are also important. Morning routines help you to set your day up for success, spiritually and mentally. Evening routines give you the time to sit and think about, and identify what you are proud of for the day and what you have accomplished. And even if you feel like you didn't accomplish anything, more than likely you were resting, and you probably needed the rest. We often forget that we are human beings and we think that we are built to go, go, go. Sometimes we do not realize that our body is going to tell us, "we're going to take a rest". So even if you feel like you did not do anything, you are probably resting, which is a form of self-care. You are entitled to a break.

There are different areas of freedom you will experience in your life. They are spiritual, emotional, freedom from others, freedom from your fears, and freedom from your past mistakes. I want you to explore each one of these below. Complete an internal self-check to see which areas you need to grow in.

Spiritual Freedom

What keeps me grounded is believing in something bigger than myself. I personally believe in energy and the universe. Believing the Universe has my back has helped me through my hard time. The more faith and believe I have, the more it shows up in my life. Having faith in something beyond myself has really helped to pull me out of what felt like a **very deep** black hole. Thinking about the people who care about me, thinking about how many people I would affect, and all of the other things that could change and open up (that were good), as a result of trusting the process caused me to hold on and fight.

Have you ever thought to yourself that you were made to do something bigger than what you're doing right now? Have you ever considered how amazing your life would be if you lived it from a place of love? When you realize your life has purpose and meaning, your attitude, your actions and more importantly your mind shifts. Out with the toxic thoughts and behaviors and in with the new self-love, acceptance of yourself, and clarity. I invite you to shift from existing to living. Take some time to identify what freedom looks like for you. If you had no limitations what would your life look like? I ask this, but the truth is there are no limits to your life. You are as free as you believe you are. It is up to you to discover and then live in your freedom. Make a freedom declaration to yourself. Speak it to the Universe. Live it, do it, and be it!

Emotional Freedom

Emotional freedom is mastering the ability to recognize and identify emotions, being able to handle them and manage them well, and being able to cope with them and move through them with ease and grace. Feeling and experiencing total freedom from people, places, and things is emotional freedom. In emotional freedom you have the ability to fully and genuinely detach from external things, with love.

Freedom From Others

Freedom from others is being able to create happiness and/or joy without needing to rely on anyone to experience it. Freedom from others is feeling secure in ourselves – in our lives, in our soul, and in our human body. It is being able to feel confident in our choices and our decisions, without needing the approval, guidance, or validation of others. Freedom from others is also recognizing that when other people are upset or bothered by us, it is more of a reflection of themselves and we should not take it personally. Freedom from others is having the ability to not be bothered or offended by anyone because we understand that if we are, it is a reflection of wounds that still need healing.

Freedom From Your Fears

Freedom from your fears comes from recognizing that fear could be a sign of growth, change, or the unknown. Fear can come from a place of being afraid to succeed – because if we succeeded that would mean we needed to show up. Fear can also arise from the thoughts of failure. If we were to shift our perception and re-mold the idea of failure to a time of practice, we would see how, over time, our fear(s) would diminish. Just like basketball players practice, musicians' practice – it is a practice to recognize our fears, realize the irrational versus rational parts of our fears, and notice how much of a [skewed] story we've created about these fears.

Freedom From Guilt of Your Past Mistakes

One of my favorite books that I recommend to my clients is "Codependent No More" by Melody Beattie. In her book and workbook, she walks the reader through working the "12-Steps of Codependents Anonymous." Part of the 12-Steps is a process of making a moral inventory of ourselves. The intention here is to acknowledge and clear our past in order to make room to create a new present (and therefore future) for ourselves. An analogy I've heard made in past workshops is to consider a bucket of muddy water. In order to get the mud out we need to put a hose in the bucket and pour clean water in. The muddy water will stir up a bit but eventually with enough clean water, the muddy water will pour over the bucket and you'll eventually have a bucket of clean water. What does all this mean? Before we can go creating new for ourselves, let's take a moment to acknowledge negative behaviors (decisions, emotions, etc.) we may have engaged in. Let us acknowledge the "mud" in the bucket, the dark, the shadow in order to clear it and make space (mental, emotional, and spiritual, etc.) for the new we would like to call in to our lives. After this process is done, then we make it a daily habit to notice when we engage in our old negative behaviors and quickly acknowledge it. Imagine how much easier it is to maintain a space that has been deeply cleaned already. Think of it as "keeping your side of the street clean."

F.R.E.E.D.O.M.

"*Fearlessly Rise up with Ease and Excitement, and Dedicate yourself to seizing Opportunities that life presents with Momentum.*"

— Dani La Barrie

Chapter Recap

Have you thought about who you need to forgive? Make amends to? Have you truly forgiven yourself?

What are your beliefs in a Higher Power, or something greater than yourself? What is your spiritual health like? If you have trouble with believing in a Higher Power/God, are you open to your Higher Power being mother nature? The Universe? Your Highest Self? I strongly encourage having a Higher Power that is to your understanding.

On the topic of gratitude, how can you pause and truly connect with all that you currently have right now in your life? If you seriously took a moment to embody gratitude, put yourself in a place of imagining what it would be really like if you lost some of the most valuable people and things in your life – what/who all are you grateful for?

Have you set gratitude alarms throughout your day to remind you to be grateful?

What are your morning and evening routines? How do you set your day up for success?

CHAPTER 9
THE OTHER SIDE

"Breathe. Let go. And remind yourself that this very moment is the only one you know you have for sure."

— Oprah Winfrey

I remember sitting in the hair salon back in 2012 for my annual birthday haircut. My hairdresser and I were talking about life – the normal spill all your business while someone massages your hair kind of talk. I told her about how bummed out I had been because the relationship I was in had gone south and the friends had ex-communicated me because I no longer wanted to drink and do drugs, and it was weird. Somewhere between the hair washing station and blow dryer, I aired out everything I had been holding inside. I talked about my fears and the insecurities while she listened attentively; it was like she was my therapist. The Universe knew I needed someone to talk to. I was so glad someone was finally listening.

That was an interesting time for me because everything in my life, besides my hairdresser was unfamiliar to me. I was in a city where I barely knew anyone. I was a little country girl living in a big place and I was like a fish out of water. I felt like crap every day and I just hated the journey. I wanted more, but I did not know how to do it or where I should go or even how to create it. I questioned my move daily – should I go back, or should I stay? During one of my rants I told her, "Yeah so, I'm checking out these yoga classes now." It was a new world, but yoga was really starting to help me gain some control and clarity. Those first months in yoga were difficult, but she encouraged me to stick with it and it would all work out. She was right. I was just going through friend's withdrawal, and I don't even know if that's a thing or not, but the loneliness was kicking my butt. Somehow, I pulled it together. I was determined to keep going.

After many self-talks, motivational podcasts, and party of one pep rallies I managed to wake up each day – one step at a time – one good choice at a time and I overcame that slump. Just like she told me, it surely paid off.

That decision to take control of my life continues to pay off today as I spread happiness around the globe. A few months ago, I had the pleasure of attending an event with my mastermind in Mexico. For a weekend I connected and bonded with other successful women who are connected to their spirituality like me. I felt liberated and "at home" to have found a group of women who are further along in their journey and can offer me wisdom and guidance as I continue to grow. I always encourage my clients to have a support system, and I share with them how even I have a support system. The feeling of belongingness is very real. I felt accepted and "normal" from being around other people who were in alignment with my values and beliefs. I did not want the weekend in Mexico to end. I was surrounded by the ocean of positive women while doing what I love. I would have never experienced this life had I not walked away from my toxic old self. I would have never discovered this new family that loves and supports me and challenges me to elevate and be a better Dani.

Leap. Connect. Align

Reaching this place of freedom in my life has allowed me to experience what life is like on the other side. It's been filled with joy, connection, and pure authenticity. It feels good when you can say you genuinely love yourself. And it

109

feels even better when you are totally unafraid of being 100% who you are…not caring what other people think of you because you love yourself so much. It truly doesn't matter how other people feel about you. It also feels amazing when you know yourself so well, you know how to self-soothe, you no longer need to rely on anyone or anything else – you learn what works and what doesn't work. It is fulfilling when you have the ability to stay grounded inside of your mind and soul regardless of what's going on around you.

I have discovered some new things about myself on this journey. I have discovered that I am stronger than I had realized before. I have discovered how much my childhood affected how I operated as an adult. I have discovered how impactful my thoughts and feelings are on my behavior. I learned that I have an inner child in me who needs to be acknowledged and to feel like she is heard. I have discovered how effective it is for me to name that ego and converse with myself the same way I would converse with a best friend (a.k.a. Self-talk).

I worked with a client, Karen, who had an addiction to drugs. In our time of working together, she was able to identify the things that triggered her and how she could respond better to them. She was open and receptive to trying out new things. She could not manage to keep a job because her partying habits would get the best of her. In working together, she learned skills and tools that helped her balance her life and her emotions. Towards the end of our working together, we also worked on challenges she was having with her boyfriend, who also had challenges with addictions. Today they are both doing well, have a home together, they both work and they are balancing their life by managing their stress. They both have support systems in place and meet regularly with accountability coaches. They are relieved they are no longer chained to bad/unhealthy habits. I am so proud of them and the tremendous commitment they have made to their journey. They have experienced life on the other side.

Gradual and Consistent Change

The truth is…and I don't want to sound like a salesperson from Disneyland but I am really enjoying my life. I would have never thought that I could laugh so much and smile so big…and it is genuine. When I think about how bad I used to feel when I would wake up from a hangover to how I feel now, there is no comparison. I would never want to go back. I am happy with my life. The change has been gradual yet consistent for me. To get myself out of what I felt was a black hole, I had to begin attending events that dealt with my mind, body, and soul. By going to holistic events and events on natural ways of health and wellness, I learned how to better take care of myself and give my body the fuel and stamina it needed. As I would attend these events, as a bonus I would meet new people and try new things. As I kept trying new and different activities, I realized how my mood and mental health started improving – *I felt better.* I noticed that I felt a lot more grounded. And that is because I slowly changed my environment. I slowly moved to a city where I did not know anybody. I slowly started making new friends and I started just doing the things that I found were happy, fulfilling, and fun. Those slow and gradual changes were the foundation to my new life and my new world.

No Guilt. No Sabotage

One of the other things that I have noticed about myself is that I rarely feel guilty or shameful about my choices. I take full ownership of what I do, and I do not spend much time trying to explain what I do to anyone. This is so different from the old Dani who constantly would apologize to others and struggled with guilt and self-sabotage all the time. I can honestly say this is because of my new self-awareness. I used to do things to please others or receive approval from other people. I also used to blame the world and felt like life was happening to me. I had not practiced taking accountability nor had I practiced not being a victim anymore. I took on a perspective of being the creator of my life and of my reality. Do not get me wrong, I have my days – where I'm learning the skill of patience and that I don't always get what I want when I want it. But for the most part, I have shifted my thinking from less of a victim to more of a creator. I do not entertain the negative voices who would want to define who they think I should be.

Fulfillment and Purpose

I am so blessed that the Universe has given me unlimited opportunities to serve women and see their lives past their current circumstances. This is what I was created to do. For over 11 years I have been helping women stop filling soul-cravings with things like unhealthy relationships, alcohol, drugs, depression, anger, and chaos, and to get FREE from unhelpful affinities. Every day I feel great knowing that I have served and given my best. If I can help more women see there is more to life than how they have been living I am in alignment with my purpose.

Just Do it

Moving to a different city where I didn't know anyone may sound a little scary, but it helped me in that I didn't know anyone to be able to find drugs anymore; I no longer had access to it. I never looked for drugs; I never went out and sought it out. Usually the people I was with had them so when I was not with those people anymore, I did not use. I did the things that made me uncomfortable and sometimes I felt like I stuck out like a sore thumb – but it also gave me a new challenge and I needed that. When I tried different activities like meditation, yoga, sound bowl healing, etc. I tried them with an open mind. Some things worked out great, others did not but I felt positive saying I at least tried something different and I was able to figure out what I liked and what I did not. I got into the habit of getting to know myself – dating myself. I encourage my clients to get on a path of getting introspective and building self-awareness. For so long, deep down inside I wanted "it" and I knew that I wanted "it", but I did not know what "it" even was. Getting in tune with myself helped me to discover "it".

Taking Responsibility for Your Choices

I look at "taking responsibility for choices" more so as being the author of my life. Any time things are chaotic in my external world, I pause and look at what is going on inside (inside my head, inside my heart, inside my soul). I am a huge believer that our external world reflects what's going on inside our head/soul. For example, if my business is disorganized and chaotic, more than likely my home life is disorganized and chaotic, and more than likely there is something going on underneath this – stress, anxiety, depression. Once I started taking accountability for my life and my choices, I also learned how to create "home" and stability inside of my head and my soul. Doing this helps me with the ability to stay grounded and calm, regardless of what is going on around me. The more I practice this, along with healthy detachment, and deepening my spiritual relationship with my Higher Power, the better I can manage my emotions.

This does not mean I will not ever experience emotions such as pain, hurt, anxiety, and sadness; this isn't about not experiencing the emotion, this is about learning how to manage and cope with the emotion(s). I use this example with my clients. We are on a boat together, and it's about learning how to manage the boat through a thunderstorm in the ocean. We cannot control the storms we go through in our boat. But we can control the boat; we can control how we get through the storm. Sometimes the storms are really, really challenging. Sometimes the storms can be so consuming that we may want to just capsize the boat and give up. But it is so important to remember that the storm does eventually pass…it cannot rain forever. If we can manage the boat enough to remember that and get through to when the rain passes, we have learned to manage our emotions.

Can you see yourself on the other side of where you are now? If we can manage the boat enough to remember that the storm does eventually pass, we have learned to get to the other side, and we have learned to manage our emotions. Emotions and thoughts are underestimated. They are such powerful forces. The stories we create in our mind and then the emotions that follow can completely influence, impact, and determine our actions, decisions, and behavior patterns. Affirmations and the practice of visualizing/visualization are key components to managing the emotions and the boat during the storms along with practicing shifting doubtful thoughts you know do not serve you.

Dare to Live Freely! Break Free From Unhealthy Behaviors and Begin Living Your Joy

– Saturated Life!

Chapter Reflections

- What are some small, gradual changes you are open to making, that you feel you can be consistent with?

- It's best to have small, attainable goals rather than large, possibly unattainable goals, so that you can build on your momentum as you achieve them. (Hanging our hat where we can't reach it can fuel discouragement and may lead you to shut down or give up easily).

- How can you shift from a victim to an author/creator of your life?

- Where can you begin taking accountability for your choices and actions?

- Even becoming aware of the choices we make in who we allow into our spaces makes a difference. Shifting from accusing others, to taking accountability in what role we played in the situations we're in.

CHAPTER 10
BUILDING NEW
HEALTHY
RELATIONSHIPS

"Do not bring people in your life who weigh you down. And trust your instincts...good relationships feel good. They feel right. They don't hurt. They're not painful. That's not just with somebody you want to marry, but it's with the friends that you choose. It's with the people you surround yourselves with."

— Michelle Obama

My idea of a fairytale romance ended with a string of failed attempts as a hopeless romantic. I ended my engagement with the kindest guy just five months before our wedding. I broke up with another guy who gave me a promise ring. And I ended a six year relationship with a man after we had made life goals on a journey we did not intend to build together. I have had my share of rocky relationships and most times I was a victim to my own low self-esteem and sabotaging thoughts which caused me to choose men that were not the best fit for me. I went into the relationship with no idea of what I wanted; I just knew I didn't want to be alone (*Mistake # 1*). I did not know myself and I changed myself to adapt to each man I dated (*Mistake # 2*). I said and did things I did not mean. If he said he wanted to do an activity – I said I wanted to do it too (*Mistake # 3*). I relied heavily on my boyfriend for my happiness. (*Mistake # 4*). Being in relationships used to be so exhausting. I put the pressure on myself to settle down in a committed relationship and have children like all my friends and to beat the biological clock that was (and still is) ticking. Most guys I dated were not the right fit for me, and things got abusive at times. I never saw the signs of course, until it was too late. By the time I realized he wasn't for me, I had already been significantly invested in the relationship making it harder for me to leave. I cannot deny there weren't signs there, I just didn't want it to end so I ignored them. My parents have been married forever, and I thought it would happen for me the way it happened for them, but it has not. Even today I must trust that when the time is right, the Universe will send me the right man that is a perfect fit for me.

Unhealthy is Normal For Some

It's interesting how most people I work with come from what society calls "a dysfunctional family". These dysfunctional environments can include parents that are divorced, instances of domestic violence, alcohol or drug abuse, emotional or sexual abuse, however, that isn't my backstory. My parents never argued in front of me – not once. If they were not getting along, I had no idea of it. I think because of this, I may have created this idea that relationships did not involve disagreements. Relationships are challenging. Relationships take a commitment to communicating and working as a team to solve the problem at hand. Without understanding what it entails to create a healthy relationship, it is easy to mistake unhealthy relationships for healthy ones.

Signs of an Unhealthy Relationship

Codependency: I have been very guilty of this one in the past. I did not have any friends and was overly, extremely attached to the person I dated. I made minimal effort in doing my own things or making new friends. I latched on to that person and sometimes they latched on to me as well…making minimal effort to have their own friends and life.

Always Having a Bag Packed or Being Ready to Leave: After watching so many romance movies, I really thought that relationships were supposed to be perfect. Any time there was any disagreement, I was ready to run. I was always ready to quit and go somewhere new. Unfortunately, this is a huge sign of unhealthiness. It shows that we are not willing to attempt to solve a problem. Now, I am in no way saying to stay in a relationship if there is any type of abuse. What I am saying though, is that relationships are not like the movies.

Constant Toxic Cycles: It can become overbearing when a bad relationship completely takes over your life, your health, and your sanity. Only you will know that – you know your limits but in every relationship you must have boundaries. When I realized my relationships weren't changing, and I finally decided to listen to that little voice inside that knows there's more to life than this, that's when I discovered me.

There was more to my life and I knew I deserved better and so do you. We cannot allow ourselves to stay in relationships that do not bring us closer to our purpose in life. If you know you need to exit a relationship, do it. Remember, you are strong enough to carry yourself and the only person that can save you is you. If you are in an unhealthy relationship you know what you need to do. So pull yourself up by the bootstraps, wipe your tears away, and take some deep breaths. It is time for you to make a commitment to date yourself. Maybe even marry yourself. It is time for you to love yourself and get to know yourself again. This is the awakening that every woman needs. Life is full of options so there is no reason for you to settle in a place where you are not happy.

The Fear of Starting Over

Trisha was in a relationship for about five years and was entertaining thoughts of leaving her boyfriend. When we met, she told me about her complicated relationship and how she was tired of the way he treated her. Trisha complained that she had been in this relationship for so long, it was difficult for her to break-up with him despite her knowing how unhealthy it was. On weekends, and sometimes during the week she would abuse cocaine and ecstasy with him. She knew he was a bad influence, but she talked herself into staying. Trisha shared that she didn't have any friends of her own because she moved to the city that her boyfriend grew-up in, and after she moved, she had a difficult time making friends outside of her relationship. They lived together and he isolated her away from her family and friends. "Isolation and domestic abuse cannot be separated. Whether physical or emotional or both, isolation is the first step to convincing a victim that their controller is the most important person in the world." *Healthyplace.com*.[14] Trisha and her boyfriend would get into arguments that involved pushing each other, choking, and one time he spat in her face. She was extremely unhappy even though her friends and family, and pretty much everyone she knew thought she was happy and things in her relationship were perfect. She wanted to leave but because she was financially dependent on him, she did not know how.

Once she made a decision that she was ready for change we started working together in identifying specific goals Trisha had, and slowly but surely marked them off her list. She was an example of a woman that when she looked in the mirror, she did not see her worth. Trisha was smart and a budding entrepreneur, but she constantly found herself putting her dreams on hold to take care of everyone else. She felt so unfulfilled in life and she did not know why she kept attracting the same type of man. I counseled Trisha and advised her that until she began to genuinely love herself, she would continue to attract men that did not love her. Her life was an outer reflection of an inward struggle. Over time we were able to uncover that diamond inside her. She started to see herself from a different lens. She began to rewrite her story and love herself first.

Like so many other women, she was afraid of the change of starting over. She told herself the lies; "He's all I have…I can't do any better than this…being with him is better than being alone." She allowed the fear of what could be to keep her stuck where she was. Her story is not unfamiliar. She was addicted to a man who did not value or appreciate who she was. A different type of addiction, but an addiction nonetheless. Although she did not admit this to me, something in her past caused her to think so low of herself that she stayed with him even after the abuse. Thankfully, Trisha's story has a great ending. Eventually the time came when she was faced with a decision to stay in that relationship or free herself from the broken cycle. Trisha decided to free herself and moved to a new city, made new friends, and to this day is managing her life well.

After working with her I realized that many women fear starting over. As humans we fear change but sometimes change is the one thing we need to get us on the right path. For me, the change of people in my circle and the environment around me was the best decision I could have made. When I moved to Palm Beach, Florida, I had a chance to have a clean slate to start over, make new friends and explore new opportunities. I was leaving a co-dependent relationship, where I made his friends my friends rather than having a life and friends of my own that I spent time with. I did not want to run the risk of running into my past at the grocery store or gym, so I moved to a new city where I did not know anyone. I also felt it was necessary to move because where I was living was meant more for families. I wanted to live in an area that was not too busy, but had things going on which would distract me from being a single 30-year-old woman with no kids. Eventually, I started checking out events that interested me, and going and doing things that made me happy. I kept meeting new people and making new friends, and I engulfed myself into personal growth and development trainings, listening to podcasts, reading books, exercising, and eating better. I made these gradual changes and now I am so happy with my life and how far I have come.

Know What You Want

Dealing with relationships can be a sensitive subject for most people. Building a healthy relationship with the new you is essential. But first it begins with knowing what you want. It is okay to have a checklist and stand firmly for what you will or will not accept in a relationship. Now I will say be flexible – what you desire may not show up in your life exactly how you pictured it, sometimes we are presented things even better than we had imagined. I want you to re-evaluate where you are and where you want to go. What are some of the traits you look for in a healthy relationship? If you have never thought about it before now would be a good time to consider it.

Traits of a healthy relationship are:

- Good communication.

- A person that encourages you to be yourself.

- Someone you can have fun with – and enjoy life.

- Someone who believes in you and shows it.

- A person who makes time to spend with you and shows you how much you mean to them.

- Someone that challenges you to be the best version of yourself.

- Someone that does not lie and sneak around on you.

These are just some traits, but of course there are others. Think about what is on your list. Out of the list above, which ones are most important to you? After you are clear about what you want, avoid anything and anyone that reminds you of the things that keep you in a toxic cycle. Yes, this is easier said than done, but if you follow the tips and strategies that I have outlined in this book, you will be better prepared to make the best decision about your life and in your relationships.

Building New Relationships

Can I let you in on how I build new relationships? I connect, communicate, and I build new relationships by really listening to what the other person is saying and tuning into how they are feeling while they are saying it. People feel good when they know they are heard. I feel good when I know I have made the connection. I find that listening and being more attentive really helps me to connect; and for me, it comes from a place of authenticity.

Building the right relationships should feel good to you when the connections are on the same frequency. Building new and healthy relationships will also keep you on target to pursuing your goals. When your relationships are healthy, you will feel different. You will do things like going out for a walk, meditating, journaling, stretching, doing some deep breathing, doing something creative, decluttering your workspace, organizing where you live, cleaning out your closet, and getting rid of things you don't use. I encourage you to try a new physical exercise or just try something new. Or even do something you have been meaning to do but maybe you have been putting it off. Once you learn how to have healthy relationships and you have broken through the unhealthy habits, you will need to fill that space up with positive people and positive activities.

I am sure it goes without saying that just because you are in a better place it does not mean you will *only* attract people that have your best interest in mind. Not everyone may have the best intentions despite yours. Pay attention to how you feel when you are around the person. If it is right, you will feel good and you will not have to force anything. But if you do not feel good about the connection, follow your intuition and don't pursue things any further.

Healthy Boundaries

It is important to evaluate how you are being treated by other people and set your boundaries if they don't handle you with care. Be even more cautious if you have recently exited a relationship as this is the time when you will be more vulnerable. I am not saying you will never be mistreated again, even as you set your boundaries there will be people that will try to cross them. No matter who it is, stand firm in the boundaries you have set and be aware of your interactions. Pay attention to the cues, triggers, and actions of others, these new relationships will be based on the new woman you are evolving into.

Cheers to the new!

Chapter Reflections

- Have you identified what you desire in a healthy relationship? And are you aware of what you don't desire?

- What do you value most in your relationships?

- Are you ready to let go of the unhealthy relationships in your life? (Breaking toxic cycles) If not, have you come to terms with doing the same thing over and over again, is not going to create different results?

- What are some new things/activities you are willing to try? Or what are some things you have been meaning to do but maybe you have been putting them off?

- Healthy boundaries: Practice saying "no" when you mean "no" and "yes" when you mean "yes", rather than agreeing to do things you may not actually want to do but feel guilty telling the person "no".

- Observe who you allow into your space.

CHAPTER 11
THE BEAUTY OF YOU

"She's a beautiful bad ass.

An angel raising hell.

A force that can't be stopped.

She is you."

Rh Sin

ey Pretty Lady, we started this journey together by taking a look in the mirror. I am hopeful by now you have decided to make some intentional changes and adjustments to how you have been treating yourself as well as how you have been allowing others to treat you. At this point I hope you have forgiven yourself and the people that have hurt you. I hope you have learned how to control your emotions and follow your heart. You are worthy of everything the Universe has to offer. You are an amazing soul that matters. No matter what the past looks like, from today I want you to begin to see the beauty of who you are. No matter how you may feel about your outward appearance, I encourage you to get comfortable in your skin. Have the intention of being unapologetic about your flaws. Exude the vibe of accepting yourself as you are.

I invite you to always love yourself just the way you are. As women we are unnecessarily hard on ourselves and it stems back to when we were kids. You read my stories earlier, so I am not exempt from this statement either. If our bodies could talk they would tell us to stop being so mean to ourselves. Well, actually our bodies do talk in a language that many people miss. When our bodies are sad – it shows up as depression. When our body is tired, it shows up in lack of focus. When our body is happy, it shows up in a smile. What is your body saying to you? Are you in a better place now than when we started on this journey together? I hope so.

One of the most important things I hope you take away from this book is that the path that you are on right now is your beautiful story. Sure there are some bumps and some cliffhangers, but if you will just keep going you are bound to bump into the beauty of who you are. If you join arms and find your tribe you will accomplish so many feats...reflect on the chapter about healthy relationships and new beginnings – now is the time to put this into action.

As you have read my story you know this has not been an easy journey. There were nights of arguing, yelling, pushing in a relationship sprinkled in here or there. Nights of cocaine, amusement, and what felt like joy, immediately followed by pure sadness, emptiness, and bewilderment. There were days of yoga fests and beach parties, to nights of throwing-up on the side of the road, not remembering my address, and keeping a duffle bag packed at all times. Over the years I have changed my outlook about how I love and honor myself. The definition of self-love is different for everyone. The way I celebrate the beauty of me is by spending time with myself – taking myself out for a dinner date and movie, or going to the beach by myself while enjoying my own company. People laugh when I attend workshops and I say, "I am dating myself". It is my truth and I am not embarrassed to say I am dating Danila and getting to know her. I am getting to know what triggers her, what upsets her, what appeases her, and what soothes her. I have some of the best dates with myself and I enjoy being with me – you should try it. I make an appointment to honor my light and the beauty of who I am.

True love first begins from within. You may choose to celebrate yourself differently as we each get to define what self-love is to us. Maybe your idea of self-love is spending time walking in the park, participating in a team sport – or even knitting. It does not matter what you do. It just matters that you do it. As long as you are not abusing yourself, just create the time for you. Make the time for you before you do anything else. Put yourself first on your to do list. We all know the dreaded to do list that never gets finished. If you keep putting yourself at the bottom of that list, you will never take care of yourself. Women have a higher rate of stress related illnesses because of this, they do not take care of their bodies until it is too late. We have this tendency to pour from an empty cup. My advice to you is to fill up your cup so it overflows and there will be no resentments in your life.

"I've died a thousand deaths, each time reinventing myself brighter, stronger, and purer than before. From the midst of destruction, I became the creator of myself. From the midst of darkness, I became my own source of light." — Cristen Rodgers

Another action I have implemented is keeping track of how I accomplished self-care that day. This is something I would suggest you add to your daily routine. I have noticed that making a regular habit of writing down the things that I have accomplished, motivates me to keep moving and do more the next day. Some days I accomplish more than others, but I do not stop. If you do it when you feel inspired, you will notice that when you do it you feel good about yourself and it keeps you grounded. Acknowledging your wins keeps you practicing the skill of mindfulness, being in the present moment, and gratitude. As you put your brain, your body and your soul into that energy space, you put back out into the universe an energy of gratitude for all that you already have, which leads you to attracting positive things, people, and experiences back into your life. It also elevates our mood when we think about the things that we have accomplished.

Exercise

Think of how a butterfly begins as a cocoon. Visualize yourself where you started and the woman you are now.

- Who do you see now?

- What epiphanies have you had?

- What changes can you begin to make?

- What changes have you already made?

- Write below a "then" (your interpretation of yourself before reading this book), and a "now" (awareness you have gained since reading) below.

We as women have such a uniqueness and level of resilience about ourselves, that no matter what we endure, we can always find our wings. We all have a shadow side and even though it may feel like you're in quicksand at times, and everything around you is caving in, there is an inner being inside of you that knows, it's a matter of getting out of our own way to access it. Many of us have lost touch with our intuition and we have become heavily reliant on technology and the advice of other people. However, we have all that we need inside of us; it is time to get in touch with your inner being…find your wings.

Chapter Reflections

- Have you been dating yourself? What kind of dates would you like to be taken on? How can you create that for yourself?

- Do not forget to make a daily list of your self-care accomplishments, so you can acknowledge yourself for taking care of you at the end of each day.

- Reminder to visualize yourself where you started and the woman you are now.

CHAPTER 12
AFFIRMATIONS

I am the queen of talking to myself and I do it quite often, I might add. I affirm to myself that I have the strength to do things even when I am extremely afraid. Self-affirmations helps me to stay strong and believe in myself. If you have tried telling yourself affirmations in the past and they didn't seem to work, pay attention to your energy while you're saying the affirmations to yourself. Affirmations can be more effective when they are emotionally charged or carry emotional weight. You need to have a strong desire for this change to happen, so every affirmation that you choose to repeat should be a phrase that is meaningful to you. For example, if you are worried about a situation and you are unsure how to handle, you can tell yourself, "I am really excited to take on new challenges."

Affirmations can look different for everyone and does not necessarily have to be the traditional "I am" statements. It is about finding what works for you. They can be said anywhere, at any time to help you get through the hard time you may be having. I suggest saying them because your words have power and affirmations distinguish our thoughts and emotions. Think about how you would want to be treated or spoken to by other people, as well as considering how you speak to a best friend of yours, this is how you should speak your affirmations to yourself. The tone in which you speak is important as affirmations help support us in self-soothing and bringing down the intense unpleasant emotions that can come along with stressful situations. When you repeat affirmations enough and believe in them, you can start to make positive changes in your life. Studies have shown how repeating affirmations can raise your confidence, improve your self-esteem, overcome a bad habit, and control unpleasant feelings such as anger, frustration, and impatience.

Affirmations promote an inner encouragement. There will be times in your life when you will be the only person cheering you on, and that is perfectly okay. You can be supportive of yourself by making sure you are saying the right things and avoiding the negative self-talk and self-sabotage. Affirmations are so important and should be said as often as possible because it is a conversation with yourself. For example, when I find myself feeling a little bit anxious or stressed out, I remind myself we are doing okay by saying,

Things are okay.

You are not going to die.

We are feeling a little scared right now because we have not done this before, or we have not been in this territory before. It is okay.

We are doing a great job.

We are doing the best that we know how to do.

I am doing my best. I have always gotten myself through things.

I can get through this. I am stronger than I think.

Other affirmations I speak to myself are:

We are going to be okay.

We are going to get ourselves out of this…we always have.

Who did we have at the end of the day? We had us at the end of the day, and we can do this.

Make sure that the affirmation is believable to your heart. If it doesn't fully feel authentic and agreeable, they won't work. This whole process is about finding what feels good for you. The same way you would not want someone to lie, exaggerate, or be inauthentic with you, is the same way you want to be authentic with yourself. So repeat affirmations that are not too far off or too much of a stretch, choose to go general and believable.

Chapter Reflections

- What are some affirmations you can create that can help you go from panic, angst, or anxiety to feeling neutral? Choose affirmations that feel authentic and genuine to you – it's easier to go from negative to neutral, than negative to positive sometimes.

- What are some rituals you are open to trying and doing to cleanse your living space of negative energy? Are you open to smudging or saging? If not, what are rituals you're open to creating for yourself? It's important to be intentional with our living space too – clearing it of negative energy.

Dear Pretty Lady,

You made it through this! How are you feeling right now? Just observe…no judgment. I acknowledge you for not only committing to yourself and investing in this book, but for seeing your commitment through by reading it to the end.

Take a moment to pause and tap into your body. What are you experiencing? How does your soul feel? What awareness and insight have you gained? What shadows did you highlight in this journey? What do you know about yourself that perhaps you did not know before? Remember, any awareness that you have gained is not to make you feel "bad" or "worse", it is just a gauge of where you have been and sheds light on the blind spots. Awareness is undervalued and underestimated; we do not know what we do not know, so when we do gain insight and awareness to our behavior that is where the magic can happen. This is where the shift and transformation occur. This is where we go from having breakdowns to having breakthroughs.

You are amazing, beautiful, and stronger than you realize. The world needs you and the world needs to see your light. We all have special gifts and talents, and we are all here for a reason. The journey does not end here, it is just the beginning to a beautiful, enjoyable life. If you have enjoyed reading this and you feel it has impacted you, then let's keep going! How can I support you in getting you to where you would like to be?

If you would like to make the jump and transform your life, I offer complimentary 30-minute discovery calls for those who are serious and READY! If this is you, send me an email Dani@DaniLaBarrie.com mentioning that you have read my book and are ready to transform your life!

Let's do this together!

Love always,

Dani

NOTES

1. Saul McLeod, "Maslow's Hierarchy of Needs," Simply Psychology, March 20, 2020, https://www.simplypsychology.org/maslow.html (accessed October 3, 2020).

2. Margaret Paul, Ph.D., "What Emotional Triggers Are + Why You Need to Understand Them," MBG Health, February 24, 2020, https://www.mindbodygreen.com/0-18348/what-are-emotional-triggers-why-you-need-to-under-stand-them.html (accessed October 3, 2020).

3. National Institute of Mental Health, Mental Illness, https://www.nimh.nih.gov/health/statistics/men-tal-illness.shtml (accessed October 3, 2020).

4. John M. Grohol, Psy.D., "Pediatrics Gets it Wrong about 'Facebook Depression'," PsychCentral, July 8, 2018, https://psychcentral.com/blog/pediatrics-gets-it-wrong-about-facebook-depression (accessed October 3, 2020).

5. Alyssa Valentin, "Are Social Media and Depression Linked? Why?," Behavioral Health of the Palm Beaches, Inc. , May 16, 2020, https://www.bhpalmbeach.com/are-depression-and-social-media-usage-linked (accessed October 3, 2020).

6. Marcia Reynolds, Psy.D., "5 Steps for Managing Your Emotional Triggers," Psychology Today, July 8, 2015, https://www.psychologyto-day.com/us/blog/wander-woman/201507/5-steps-managing-your-emotional-triggers (accessed October 3, 2020).

7. Substance Abuse and Mental Health Services Administration, The NSDUH (National Survey on Drug Use Health) Report https://www.samhsa.gov/data/sites/default/files/NSDUH-SR200-RecoveryMonth-2014/NSDUH-SR200-Recovery-Month-2014.htm (accessed October 3, 2020)

8. Hokuma Karimova, MA, "The Emotion Wheel: What It Is and How to Use It," Positive Psychology, January 9, 2020, https://positivepsychology.com/emotion-wheel (accessed October 3, 2020).

9. Danielle West, "You Have 34,000 Emotions You Could Experience!," Intentional Marriages, September 26, 2018, https://intentionalmarriages.net/34000-emotions-experience/ (accessed October 3, 2020).

10. Hilary Stokes, Ph.D. & Kim Ward, Ph.D., "Emotions Are Energy: The body mind connection and emotion," Authenticity Associates, August 28, 2012, https://www.authenticityassociates.com/emotions-are-energy (accessed October 3, 2020).

11. Jessica Stillman, "5 Steps to Get the Right Mindset for Success," Inc.com, January 29, 2015, https://www.inc.com/jessica-stillman/5-steps-to-get-the-right-mindset-for-success.html (accessed October 3, 2020).

12. Melissa Chu, "Why Your Environment is the Biggest Factor in Changing Your Life," Inc.com, August 21, 2017, https://www.inc.com/melissa-chu/its-possible-to-design-your-environment-to-help-yo.html (accessed October 3, 2020).

13. Oxford University Press (2020) freedom. In: Lexico.com, Available at: https://www.lexico.com/en/definition/freedom (accessed October 3, 2020).

14. Kellie Jo Holly, "Isolation and Domestic Abuse: How Abusers Isolate Victims," Healthy Place, November 6, 2011, https://www.healthyplace.com/blogs/verbalabuseinrelationships/2011/11/isolation-is-key-for-the-ability-to-abuse (accessed October 3, 2020).

ABOUT THE AUTHOR

Dani La Barrie is a virtual licensed psychotherapist. Dani is from 'little ol' Homestead, Florida. She is a successful entrepreneur and a Happiness Transformation Coach who specializes in helping ambitious people break through unwanted habits. Having professional and personal experience with mental health and addiction for the last 12 years, Dani is excited to bring it all to the mainstream with her private practice, seminars, retreats, books, Cacao Ceremonies, and speaking engagements.

Website: www.DaniLaBarrie.com

Social media:

Facebook.com/DaniLaBarrie

Instagram.com/DaniLaBarrie